HOUSE + LOVE = HOME

HOUSE + LOVE = HOME

CREATING WARM, INTENTIONAL SPACES FOR A BEAUTIFUL LIFE

JENNY MARRS

WITH SPECIAL APPEARANCES BY DAVE MARRS

CO-HOSTS OF *FIXER TO FABULOUS*

CONVERGENT
NEW YORK

Published in the United States by Convergent Books,
an imprint of Random House, a division of
Penguin Random House LLC, New York.

CONVERGENT BOOKS is a registered trademark and its C colophon
is a trademark of Penguin Random House LLC.

Photo and illustration credits begin on page 240.

Hardback ISBN 9780593444337
Ebook ISBN 9780593444344

Printed in China on acid-free paper

convergentbooks.com

2 4 6 8 9 7 5 3 1

FIRST EDITION

Title-page image by Adam Albright
Book design by Barbara M. Bachman

FOR MY LOVES—

DAVE, BEN, NATHAN, SYLVIE,

CHARLOTTE, AND LUKE

The ache for home lives in all of us,

the safe place where we can go

as we are and not be questioned.

—MAYA ANGELOU,
All God's Children Need Traveling Shoes

CONTENTS

OUR WORK, OUR FAMILY, OUR HOME

I'M JENNY. I'M A WIFE AND mom, a designer, a writer, and a passionate advocate for community transformation. I'm married to the most hardworking, faith-centered, kind-hearted man who happens to build houses for a living. My husband, Dave, and I live in a rescued and restored farmhouse, where we have a life full to the brim with five young kiddos, mud puddles galore, and too-many-to-count farm animals.

Since founding Marrs Developing in 2004, Dave has built and restored several hundred houses, and over the past decade we have worked together to design and create spaces that are warm and welcoming. Our company motto is the simplest of equations: *House + Love = Home*. We believe a home should reflect the personalities of the ones who live there. It should be a place where the people and the things you love surround you. Beautiful spaces are most often imperfect and full of character. Just like people. Perfection is never the goal.

Dave is an expert craftsman, builder, and general contractor. His knowledge of restoring old homes is unsurpassed, and his passion for bringing the unique qualities of historic homes back to life is contagious. His work also includes building new custom homes and renovating spaces, as well as crafting unique and gorgeous furniture. He mills his own lumber, and we partner with local artisans to ensure that each Marrs Developing home is built with the utmost quality, care, and integrity.

I support the design side of our busi-

who had recently relocated to this little corner of the world. Dave knew he wanted to build homes, and since his dad had been a builder back in Colorado, they decided to start a business together here.

We arrived with all of our earthly belongings in the back of a U-Haul and immediately got to work scouring the want ads for a place to rent. We quickly found a house and asked to see it. After the owner

ness and spend my days managing the thousands of details that go into the making of a home. I love nothing more than scouring my favorite sources for the perfect light fixtures, cabinet hardware, doors, tile, paint colors, furniture, and art. The list of choices to be made when remodeling or building a home can be overwhelming and feel endless at times. My job is to work with our homeowners to make the decision-making process less staggering. I truly love how important each step in the process is and how each detail is significant.

Although Dave is originally from Kiowa, Colorado, and I grew up in Orlando, Florida, we've called Bentonville, Arkansas, our hometown since we moved here in 2004. I still vividly remember our first home together. We had just moved to Northwest Arkansas to be near Dave's parents and brother,

of the house showed us around, we enthusiastically asked if we could move in. As in, right then. He looked out front, saw the U-Haul in the driveway, and handed us the keys. We spent the sweetest year and a half in that little house. In the almost twenty years since then, we've lived in five different homes. Our most recent move—and our last for a long time—involved relocating an old farmhouse from one side of Bentonville to the other, where we placed it on a lovely piece of land and then restored it. It's now our home and we love it here.

Dave and I are parents to five children—twin boys, Ben and Nathan; two daughters, Sylvie and Charlotte; and our most recent arrival, three-year-old Luke. Needless to say, life is busy, chaotic, and messy. But more than anything, it is abundantly joyful and full of laughter.

After family and work, our primary focus is building community in our own backyard and around the world. Our passion for furthering locally active, globally focused causes led to the founding of The Berry Farm. At its simplest, the U-pick farm and its event-space barn are a place for local families to gather and enjoy community while filling their buckets with fresh local berries.

But the real mission of The Berry Farm is a domino effect, rippling from Northwest Arkansas to Zimbabwe, where our profits help to support vocational training, farming skills, and food security for orphaned children. We are passionate about orphan care, family preservation, and adoption. Our older daughter, Sylvie, was adopted from Africa. During the lengthy and grueling process to bring her home to us at last, we met many wonderful people who are doing amazing work in Africa. More than a decade ago, we partnered with a couple, John and Orpah Chinyowa, who advocate and care for kids and families in their community in rural Zimbabwe.

In 2018, Dave and I were approached by HGTV about developing a home-renovation show. We were hesitant at first, but eventually decided to dive in, hoping that it might give us an opportunity to talk about the things we value. Together we created *Fixer to Fabulous,* a show focused on restoring homes in our beautiful Northwest Arkansas area. We're now in our fourth season, and it's been a wild ride—one that was unexpected and never on our radar, but one that has brought incredible opportunities and people into our lives, for which we are immensely grateful. We love helping people create houses that become homes with intention. We strive to create family places filled with purposeful, inviting, warm spaces where each person can exhale and rest, away from the chaos of the world.

WARM PLACES & INTENTIONAL SPACES

JENNY'S THOUGHTS ON HOW TO USE THIS BOOK

I stayed up too late last night reading a book. I didn't feel in a rush to put it down because I knew the gift that awaited me in the morning: a gloriously free schedule. However, instead of my anticipated slow-to-wake morning, my treasured sleep was interrupted by a soft whisper in my ear, "Momma, wake up." As I emerged from sleep, the whisper rose several octaves. "It snowed! It snowed!"

I jumped out of bed, grabbed my glasses, and ran hand in hand with my sweet girl to the windowsill. We peered over the edge and gasped at the unexpected thrill of freshly fallen snow. I grew up in Florida, and as a child never once had the joy of waking to a blanket of white covering the earth. To this day, I marvel when I catch the first glimpse of snowflakes swirling out of the sky. I doubt I could ever tire of the wonder and beauty of freshly fallen snow.

Dave, a natural early riser who truly doesn't understand my affinity for sleep, brought two piping-hot cups of coffee over to where Charlotte and I sat at the window. As we sipped the coffee, Dave and I talked through what needed to be done now that the snow had surprised us: There were hungry animals to feed, new hay to deliver to the pastures, and ice to be broken. I pulled down our winter coats and gloves from the closet and we set out.

My boots landed softly in the snow and a cold north wind whipped across my face as I made my way to the first pasture where our little farm menagerie lived: nine sheep (with two babies on the way), Alfie the Alpaca, Larry the Llama, and Daddy Donk the Donkey. Buckets of feed in hand, I tried to unlock the pasture fence and found it frozen. Undeterred, I climbed over the fence. Just as I set my second foot down in the pasture, I slipped on a patch of ice. I quickly grabbed hold of the fence, releasing the buckets, allowing small pellets of feed to sail through the air and scatter all over. Teddy, one of our two rams, ran my way. I smiled. *He senses something is wrong and is coming to check on his favorite shepherdess,* I thought. As I bent down to greet him, he ran past me toward the feed sprinkled over the ground. Immediately, the rest of the herd followed, and I was suddenly surrounded by animals pushing their way through to breakfast.

Daddy Donk stopped beside me for a neck rub as if to say, "I see you," before heading off to big-brother nudge Teddy out of his way.

I smiled, content. This full pasture, this farm we have cultivated, and our beloved old farmhouse are much like the overnight snow: unexpected and beautiful. Yes, the snow will eventually turn into a slushy mess. Most assuredly it will bring extra work for Dave and me. Yet, it brings so much joy: memories of sledding and building snowmen and racing inside to drink hot cocoa, warm hands, and dry boots by the fire.

The life we have built here can be messy and is certainly a lot of work, but, *gracious,* it's full of joy. Our memories have seeped into the walls, and these floors echo with the thrill of first steps and kitchen dance parties. Just as the biting cold of winter will eventually give way to the gentle warmth of spring and the sticky heat of summer, our home will continue to grow and change and evolve with the seasons of life.

Over the years, our family has grown and this home has expanded, baby gates have come and gone from the staircase, rooms have been reoriented, spaces have been carved out to accommodate homework stations and toy nooks and cushions for reading by the window. As a family of

seven in a 1903 farmhouse, we are busting at the seams. But I know the day will come—much sooner than my heart would like—when we will watch each of our babies step through the door to go build a life of his or her own out in the world. Then, our home will be quiet, and we will once again rework the spaces inside.

From the first moment I set foot in this old house, I could feel the stories it held. On that day, years ago, Dave excitedly led me from room to room, and we started dreaming about restoring her former beauty and breathing life back into her walls. For more than a hundred years, these walls have stood witness to celebrations and sorrows and first words and last breaths. That's the beauty of a home: It stands steadfastly as the whirl of life inside unfolds.

If you've lived long enough, you know antonyms like joy and sorrow coexist. The same is true for remarkable beauty and normal life. Seeking beauty is an intentional choice: We can choose to bemoan the handprints on the windowpane, or we can pause to watch as a curious toddler pounds out a rhythm on his newfound makeshift drum. We can choose to close the door, lamenting over the unused room where clutter has piled up, or we can reimagine the space and create a writing room or an art studio or a playroom for the kids. We can choose to give a foothold to shame—*our home is too small, our dishes are chipped, the bathroom remodel is still half-finished*—or we can throw open the door and fill the table with friends and serve take-out pizza on paper plates.

Dave and I have built and remodeled hundreds of homes throughout our careers, and we believe that first and foremost a home needs to function well. It needs to serve you and your family's needs. We also believe your home should be beautiful. The tricky thing here is that beauty is most assuredly in the eye of the beholder. Everyone has a different take on what makes a space appealing, and there is only one person who matters when it comes to whether or not your home is beautiful: you. If you smile while you're stirring a pot of soup on the stove, then you have a beautiful kitchen. Your home shouldn't be a reflection of the latest trends or of what I think or of what Pinterest tells you it should be; it should simply be a reflection of who you are.

The concept of home has always intrigued me. Several years ago, before moving to the farm, we lived in our town's historic downtown district. In the evenings, we would often head out our door, pushing the twins in the double stroller, and walk to the town square. I'm not sure if it was because of my natural curiosity, my obsession with all things home, or just a tendency to snoop, but I loved to walk past houses that had their curtains open and lights on, getting a glimpse of life bustling inside. It was an added bonus if the windows were ajar and I could hear the sound of laughter floating in the air or the unmistakable clink of forks on dishes. I could conjure up elaborate histories for the family inside and imagine all the characters seated around the dinner table.

Dave and I both, when drawn to a particular place while traveling, will seek out the real estate office in town and scan the homes for sale. As we look over the possibilities hung in the window, we imagine what daily life could look like in a foreign place. Because to us, home is so much more than four walls and a roof. Home isn't tied to a specific town but can exist anywhere in the world. Home is simply the collective memories created inside the walls. The old saying "Home is where the heart is" is remarkable in its simplicity and accuracy.

To me, home should feel like a warm blanket wrapped around you in the night, the place where you can feel safe and held and loved regardless of the dark world outside the window. Home is the place you are always excited to return to, even after an amazing adventure someplace new. Home beckons the soul.

I didn't want to write a standard how-to guide for decorating or renovating your home. There are enough beautiful and well-written books on the subject out there already. And, honestly, I don't believe there is a one-size-fits-all guide that accounts for personal style and preference. Instead, I want this book to encourage you to be creative with your home.

Throughout, I will share examples from our own home, as well as projects we have completed. Some of the ideas within these pages might inspire a creative Saturday afternoon project, while others may help you rethink entire spaces. I want to give you permission to step outside your comfort zone and make your home a reflection of what you love: paint the walls, tear up the carpet, install the wallpaper, buy the antique desk, hang the painting . . . take a risk.

It is important to understand the intention behind a home and each space within it before you start any remodel project. I've learned that the questions below are a good place to start when planning for any remodel, renovation, or redesign:

How do I want to feel in this space?
How do I currently use this space versus how do I hope to use this space?
How do I want my family, my friends, and my guests to feel in this space?

In the book, I've included what we call "Transformational Tips"—big-picture approaches for how to think about remaking or creating a space with intention. For some of these tips, you may need outside help, more time and/or resources. I've also added in "Jenny's Tips," which are easier to accomplish, are smaller scale, and can more quickly and inexpensively transform a space.

As you'll see, Dave also makes many special appearances, adding his own take on our life and work here in Bentonville. In "Dave's Corner," he outlines some of the more creative solutions he has developed regarding how to think about spatial and structural challenges in a home. He also shares some of the amazing things he's made over the years. We've included a few fairly simple DIY projects in case you are handy or feeling inspired.

Whether you're remodeling an entire house, redecorating a space, or building a new home from the ground up, simply remember: In your home, you should be surrounded by the people and things you love. Your people should feel welcome and safe. There should be intentional spaces carved out for the ones you cherish. And you should display the things that bring you joy. The pieces that tell your story are meaningful and beautiful and deserve to be seen. Don't overthink it. It really is that simple.

My goal for this book is not to help you turn your home into a place intended for a picture-perfect magazine or Instagram-worthy photos. Perfection is impossible when it comes to home. Because perfection is actually the antithesis of a real, well-lived-in home. But intention is very much possible. If you address each room in your home with thoughtful intentionality, you can transform any space from a place of chaos into a place of peace.

Intentionally planning a space allows it to work better for you and your family. And, most important, you can bring more personality and joy and love into the four walls of your home.

I always say that a home should be a reflection of the family that lives there, and my hope for this book is that it will inspire you to make a few simple changes that allow your home to reflect your heart.

HOUSE + LOVE = HOME

CHAPTER 1

INVITING IN

THE FRONT OF YOUR HOME, PORCHES & ENTRYWAYS

—

the Porch Swing

OUR OLDER DAUGHTER, Sylvie, is adopted. Her birth country is in central Africa and her journey into our family was tumultuous to say the least. Dave and I had to fight bureaucracy, red tape, and political posturing for two very long, very hard years to bring her home. During the wait, I spent countless hours sitting on our front porch swing, praying for her health and safety and for the miracle to take place that would finally bring her home to us.

Our porch swing was the site of every photograph that marked an important milestone during those difficult years of waiting. We have a photo of her brothers sitting on the swing, holding a sign announcing Sylvie's adoption, which we shared with the wider circles of our families.

A year or so later, Sylvie had still not reached us. Another photo: her brothers sitting on the swing, holding up a photo of her in Africa alongside an ultrasound photo of the joyful, albeit unexpected, pregnancy of her soon-to-arrive younger sister. Only three years old then, Nate and Ben were so excited by the idea of these two new sisters whom they had not yet met. Months later, as we continued to wait for Sylvie, we all sat on the swing again for a photo, this time holding our newborn daughter, Charlotte, and another updated photo of Sylvie. Finally, after 602 days of clinging to hope, our daughter arrived on U.S. soil and came to us, by which time we had moved to our current home, where we had a large porch swing built by Dave, perfect for more photographs.

As long as I live, I will never forget the thrill of that first morning with Sylvie. She and I were both restless. I eventually gave up on sleep and scooped her up, tiptoeing to the front door. I quietly turned the knob and we stepped out together onto the front porch. The sun was breaking through the horizon, as she clung to me. I took a seat on that much-used swing.

The rays of sunlight warmed my bare feet. The air was still, and the world was hushed. It seemed as if the

birds even refrained from their typical morning chatter. Time felt suspended as I held my girl and gently rocked her back and forth. We didn't speak. We simply sat together holding on to each other. She hadn't been in my arms since the summer before when I had had to leave her behind at the end of a visit. In the many months since, I had been haunted by the memory of her tears as she was ripped from my embrace in the dark, sweltering summer night back in the Democratic Republic of the Congo. I had often wondered if I would ever feel the weight of her toddler frame again. That morning, under the glow of a summer's sunrise, I rubbed her back and my tears fell. She was indeed here: This was real. The porch swing that had held so many tears of sorrow and grief and utter helplessness now held tears of sheer joy and unimaginable gratitude.

To me, the front porch isn't a space to overlook on the way into a home, it is an extension of the home itself. It's the place where I start my day, on my beloved porch swing, piping-hot coffee in hand, watching the world awaken around me. It's the place for midsummer afternoon naps, the soft breeze gently lulling me to sleep. It's the place where our family gathers at the end of a long day, our very own watchtower from which to witness the sky shift from soft hues of blue to vibrant pinks and burning reds as the sun dips below the horizon. It's the place where Dave and I will sip a glass of full-bodied red wine and listen to the high-pitched tune of the cicadas' song after tucking all the kids into bed. The rhythm of my day is calibrated by stepping out my front door and onto my front porch. I begin and end most days here and find myself exhaling with gratitude as I look out above the handrail.

Of all the beautiful places I've seen in the world, the view from my front porch will always be my favorite. I've witnessed so much change from here. We created a farm where there was once wild, unruly vines and brush. We now have a pasture full of animals and a pond they meander to throughout the day. We marvel as we watch brand-new mommas coax their shaky-legged newborn lambs to their feet. After growing up in Florida, where the seasons consisted of hot and very hot, I am constantly in awe of the beauty of this place; my view changes with the four seasons. The vibrant green of spring turns to the deep, lush landscape of summer. Fall brings golden light and changing leaves before the magical, soft, white hush of a winter's snow appears.

Yes, the kitchen is often called the heart of the home. Yet I believe the front porch is the soul. It's often more still. But if ever there were a space to represent hospitality, it is the front porch. It is the first welcoming place, a threshold to cross when entering a home. It's also a place to gather. I couldn't possibly count the number of deep, authentic conversations about community or parenting or faith we have shared with friends on our front porch.

When Dave and I first moved to our farmhouse, I felt isolated. We had been living in our town's historic downtown area, where we could easily walk to friends' houses and guests would spontaneously drop by while on a walk in the evening or for coffee in the morning. I loved it. I loved every unexpected visitor and the constant presence of our little community within the walls of our home. When we moved to the farmhouse on the outskirts of town, we were too far away for walking-past, dropping-by friends to pop over.

The days were long with a newborn, a toddler, and twin four-year-olds at home. Dave was working, building our business, while I had left my career to focus on our littles for a season. I craved adult interaction and missed having impromptu company. Our eldest daughter was newly home from the Democratic Republic of the Congo and most days our home felt like a triage center. I was juggling Sylvie's needs with the constant demands of newborn Charlotte, along with our preschool boys who had just had their entire world flipped upside down. I was burned out and certainly didn't shower consistently. Our house was never clean and laundry piles were the only constant.

The thought of inviting friends over for a dinner party seemed exhausting and absurd. Yet, one Sunday afternoon I ignored the absurdity and sent out an SOS text to three of my dearest friends. They showed up with the makings of dinner—Corrie brought a Caesar salad, Erin brought chili and fresh bread, and Melissa brought her mom's famous fudge pie and a bottle of wine. Their husbands and kids came along and, before I knew it, our home was full of laughter and the sounds of glasses clinking. We pushed aside the craft projects on the kitchen table, lit a few candles, and ladled soup into bowls. The kids went to eat on the porch while the adults sat around the table. As I lowered myself into the chair, I exhaled a sigh of deep gratitude to be gathered again with our people. That Sunday became the first of a longstanding series of Sunday dinners that lasted for years.

After dinner, we would carry our plates of dessert out to the front porch swings—we now have two—and rocking chairs. A few of us would spill over onto the stoop. The kiddos would run around in the yard, chasing after the flickering light of fireflies. Sometimes they'd be entertained by the baby lambs leaping in the pasture or by tumbling down the hay bales that they fruitlessly tried to ascend.

After the adults had settled into our seats, we would dive into stories from the past week. Most often, laughter echoed off the front wall of our home as we re-hashed the latest anecdotes of our lives. We never shied away from authenticity: Our lighthearted chatter often turned to sharing our parenting struggles or work conflicts. We were a safe space for tears when the clutches of grief gripped one of our own. We wrestled with questions of faith and prayed honest and desperate prayers together. Often Erin's husband, Zach, would strum the guitar, as together we lifted songs of praise into the star-filled night sky.

Yes, Dave and I love the look of a front porch and the character it adds to a home. But, even more, it's our attempt to recapture the spirit of slowing down and making time to nurture relationships. When Dave and I restore an old house, we always preserve the front porch.

THE COOPERS WANTED TO transform their home from a small Craftsman into a Creole cottage, inspired by their New Orleans heritage. To do so, we removed the existing gabled front porch overhang and substituted a low-hipped front porch, spanning the full width of the house. We replaced the old, rotting siding, and, most important, added four pairs of narrow French doors with custom-built shutters across the front of the home to capture the Creole cottage feel. Quintessential New Orleans–style accents like handcrafted copper gas lanterns (complete with details like a vintage fleur-de-lis locking piece), a historic front door, a blue-painted ceiling, an antique brick walkway and skirt along the house, and custom porch swings completed the look.

Doors—Colors & Materials

A front door makes a statement and is an opportunity to create a beautiful focal point for a home. A wooden front door adds warmth, while a painted front door can add contrast to the color of the exterior siding. I personally love to find an old door, strip the layers of paint off, and seal it with a water-based clear coat to preserve its natural look. Then the simple addition of a mail slot can add further character. To save money on a new front door, I like to use a less expensive fiberglass option and paint it an interesting color. A pop of color on the front door and window shutters creates instant charm.

THE OWNERS REALLY WANTED to keep the design integrity of their house's mid-century aesthetics, which we loved, and which gave us a fun creative challenge. Dave and our craftsman friend Derek built a new front door, using vertical wood slats that felt true to the house's original 1970 construction date. We then repeated the verticality throughout the entryway, even echoing it in the hallway staircase. I love when elements tie

in with one another to make a space feel cohesive. Even though these elements were all new, they complemented the aesthetic of the house, adding authenticity to the entryway.

DAVE AND I WERE honored to restore this 124-year-old home for friends of ours, the Newberrys. The house has been a part of our town for more than a century and we fell in love with its quirks and character. Restoring its original charm while updating it to accommodate a young family of five was a wonderful challenge. Dave and I wanted to incorporate as many original elements as possible back into the home, while also freshening it up. The exterior

trim had long been a bright yellow—earning the house the name "the yellow house on the corner." The house also had two front doors—one leading into the kitchen and one leading into the master bedroom.

Jenny's Tip

REUSING OLD HARDWARE AND OTHER MATERIALS

One unique feature of this house was the original hardware on the doors. The door-knob contains a built-in doorbell that still works. Our friend, local artisan Adrian (from Olde World Door & Sunshine Glass), was able to restore the original door knocker and doorbell and reinstall it on the front door. It's probably the coolest front doorknob I've ever seen.

You simply push the button that reads "push" and the internal doorbell rings. I'm sure the family's kids have had a lot of fun with that feature. For the walkway, we repurposed the brick from an old fireplace inside the house.

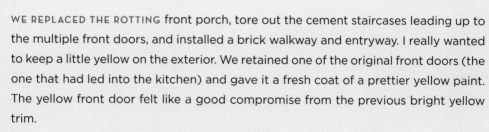

WE REPLACED THE ROTTING front porch, tore out the cement staircases leading up to the multiple front doors, and installed a brick walkway and entryway. I really wanted to keep a little yellow on the exterior. We retained one of the original front doors (the one that had led into the kitchen) and gave it a fresh coat of a prettier yellow paint. The yellow front door felt like a good compromise from the previous bright yellow trim.

Intention

ENCOURAGING COMMUNITY

Dave

Front Porch Living

ONE OF MY FAVORITE TERMS is "front porch living." Many of us live in beautiful parts of America where we have eight to nine months a year to comfortably be outdoors. Front porch living is a way to bring the living room outside—to create a welcoming place for community, a place for stories, and a place for memories, whether you're gathered around an outdoor table, sitting in rocking chairs, or relaxing on a beautiful porch swing. It's a place where life happens. You can have different conversations. You can engage in different activities. So many things can take place on a front porch that will enrich your family life and build a stronger community.

Jenny's Tip

FURNITURE PLACEMENT AND SYMMETRY
TO CREATE MULTIUSE SPACES

Determining seating and how to organize space on a porch is so important. We make sure there are areas for the many ways the homeowners hope to use their porches, whether it be for sitting, rocking, napping, lounging, or dining. We match those wishes with furniture designs that also make the most sense for the style of the house by bringing in rocking chairs, porch swings, benches, or even oversized pillows. Oftentimes just trying to figure out how we can maximize seating, while still having a porch that looks spacious and welcoming, is the biggest challenge.

I love symmetry, so whenever I can, I'll have at least two of a type of seating: two rocking chairs, two loungers, two dining chairs, two porch swings. Maximizing porch space to create beauty and symmetry, while also making the pieces adaptable enough for all sorts of front porch life, helps to create an immediate welcoming stage for the front of a home.

THIS BELOVED FARMHOUSE has been in the Crowder family for generations and is now owned by granddaughter Lisa. Lisa's dad was born and raised in the house, and she spent her childhood visiting her granny here. Preserving the essence of the home and its family history was of utmost importance. Lisa wanted more space for time with family, and a comfortable spot from which to watch storms roll in, so we expanded her outdoor living space.

TRANSFORMATIONAL TIP *Window Shutters*

A smaller project that can pay big dividends is adding window shutters. By adding, stripping, and/or painting window shutters, you can bring visual interest, symmetry, and charm to the porch and entry area of the house.

IN LISA'S WORDS, "The porch is much more functional now and super comfortable, but one of my very favorite parts about the porch . . . is just looking at it as I drive up! It's good for my mental health. We have draped outdoor lights on the porch and over our outdoor table; it is so cute at night . . . so inviting!"

THE OUTSIDE OF THE existing house had the potential to be adorable—it just needed a little sprucing up. After we stripped and stained the doors, added new cedar shutters, power washed and stained the deck, and updated the landscaping, the exterior was almost completely transformed. We also installed new brick steps and a new brick chimney and, most important, we extended the front porch to create an expanded outdoor dining space. As Lisa later wrote, what "was an unsightly spot in the yard is now valuable new porch space to use for our family dinners."

THIS 170-YEAR-OLD HOUSE predates the Civil War. The owners, Amy and Eric Duca, loved its history and character, but really wanted more of a modern style. I worked with them on design decisions that blended new ways of thinking about space and style while retaining much of the house's old charm. The house held treasures within its walls that could be found only in the craftsmanship of the nineteenth century. Its magnificent exterior Victorian details were somewhat hidden behind overgrown landscaping. We freshened up the outside to reveal the entryway and porch area. We tidied the landscaping and painted the exterior. The house already had a wonderful wraparound front porch; we rethought the seating, adding an intimate

area for eating or having tea, as well as an oversized porch swing, big enough to nap on. The period details, including the original glass-and-wood door, bell, and pocket stained-glass window, worked wonderfully with the new elements. When we were finished, the porch had become a historic treasure with a fresh update, offering a place where Amy and Eric could welcome family and old and new friends.

Oversized Porch Swing

THE DUCAS' PORCH called not only for a porch swing, but a porch swing big enough for two or three (or more) people to sit on comfortably—the one we built was twin-bed-sized! We preserved a piece of the house's history by repurposing the wooden handrails from the back porch to make the sides and back of the swing. You can take a nap on it. You can listen to the birds on it. You can hear neighborhood kids at play while swinging on it.

Dave

Jenny's Tip

PLANTERS AND WINDOW BOXES

Landscaping the front of a house can be an expensive and time-consuming project. One quicker, more affordable way to invite the natural world in to the front of your house is to add window boxes, where plants can be swapped in and out seasonally to provide color and character. Planters by the front door, whether you live in a freestanding house or an apartment building, can also bring a lovely dash of greenery and color to your entry.

CHAPTER 2

WELCOMING

THRESHOLD AREAS, HALLWAYS & DROP ZONES

—

the Paris Suitcase

N MAY 2004, I BOARDED MY FIRST international flight. Dave had surprised me the previous Christmas with the most incredible gift: tickets to Paris, France. I had long dreamed of visiting the City of Lights, exploring the ancient streets, consuming copious amounts of bread and cheese, and ascending the Eiffel Tower. Although I had never before stepped foot in Europe, I had been fascinated by all things Parisian since college. I hung framed black-and-white photos of the Eiffel Tower on the walls of my apartment and lined my bookshelves with travel books filled with Paris's must-see attractions. I listened to French music and tried, albeit unsuccessfully, to learn the language by signing up for an online course.

In the months leading up to the long-awaited trip, I started planning what I would bring. Having grown up with a mom who packed our minivan to the brim for a forty-minute drive to the beach, I packed as I always had: in a suitcase so massive that it never stood a chance of coming in under the 50-pound weight limit. I loaded my luggage with multiple shoe options, full-sized shampoo and conditioner bottles, and enough clothes for a month even though we would be gone for only two weeks. I was operating under the assumption that you could never be too prepared and apparently didn't understand that basic necessities could be found in French stores.

Dave had bigger plans for the trip than simply exploring the city with me: He was going to propose. Years before, when we were just friends and had not even begun dating, a couple of our friends got engaged and I made the offhanded comment to Dave that my dream proposal would be at the top of the Eiffel Tower. Being the romantic that he is, Dave had stored that conversation away and planned to fulfill my outlandish wish on this trip. But after dragging my massive bag through the cobblestone streets and struggling under its weight up the three flights of narrow stairs to our quaint hotel room, I'm fairly certain he questioned his intentions. Squeezing the three of us—Dave, me, and my suitcase—into that hotel room was the first challenge we faced in our relationship. We had to turn our bodies sideways, pull the suitcase through the narrow entry and, once it was in, we had to step over it to get into the room each evening.

Thankfully, Dave overlooked my irra-

tional overpacking trait and still asked me to be his wife on the third night of our trip. He had carefully planned the moment, waiting until that specific night to throw off my suspicions. That evening, we arrived at the Eiffel Tower and took the stairs halfway up, then rode the elevator the rest of the way. The elevator was crowded, and when the doors opened, we joined the masses on the outer deck of the tower, overlooking the city. Unbeknownst to me, the tower was too crowded for Dave's plan, making him anxious that his proposal was potentially unraveling.

Dave was acting strange, but I was too caught up in the moment to really consider what was going on with him. At one point, I went to hold his hand and he practically jumped out of his skin. I chalked it up to the possibility that he was afraid of heights, too lost in the expansive view to give rise to my own fears. It was a perfect evening; the sky was clear, and the view was nothing short of magical.

We descended the tower and took the obligatory tourist photos below. I wasn't ready to step out of the enchantment of the night and, as we stood there, looking up at the glow of the lights against the clear, dark sky, Dave turned to me and said, "Marry me," in a voice mimicking a popular commercial at the time. I laughed and said, "But of course!" To which he replied, "I'm serious." And in what can only be described as an out-of-body experience, I watched as he dropped to one knee and held up a small box containing my engagement ring. I screamed with delight and grabbed him by the neck, partially choking him. He picked me up and swung me around, before placing the ring on my finger.

As we toasted and sipped our bubbly champagne later that evening, I asked Dave how he knew I had always secretly dreamed of a proposal at the Eiffel Tower. He reminded me of our conversation years earlier in which I'd mentioned it. I had completely forgotten, and couldn't believe he had tucked my words away for so long. All these years later, I continue to be in awe of and grateful for the way Dave pays attention to the little details and loves so extravagantly.

After our time in Paris, we took a train to Nice and quickly learned that we should have purchased an extra ticket for my suitcase. It took up more than half of the small sleeping cabin we had booked. When we stepped off the train and into the warm Mediterranean sunshine, beads of sweat instantly appeared on Dave's forehead as he heaved

the infamous luggage down the train platform. Once again, we performed the enormous-suitcase-that-doesn't-fit-into-a-tiny-French-hotel-room dance as we checked in to yet another quaint room. At this point, the situation was genuinely comical, and I vowed to never again lug around so much stuff.

We still look back on that trip with such joy and laughter when remembering my behemoth luggage. These days, I travel with one small carry-on and have mastered the art of packing light.

Several years ago, we traveled as a family of six to South Africa for an entire month and I packed everything we needed in one suitcase. I deemed it packing redemption and was deservedly quite proud. Over time, I have not only changed my ways when it comes to packing but I have also learned to be hypercritical of every purchase I make and every item I bring into our home. I never want to settle into a lifestyle of excess and accumulation that is often commonplace in our culture. Most important, I want to model intentional simplicity for my children so that they can grow up to be good humans who value people and relationships over things.

During that South Africa trip, I was able to spend time in a small village in neighboring Zimbabwe, visiting our dear friends and nonprofit partners, Pastor John and his wife, Orpah. I can't recall ever meeting a more God-fearing, joyful-despite-circumstances, and humble husband-and-wife team. They are truly living in the center of God's will and call on their lives, and their smiles, warm embraces, and genuine compassion are contagious. When I stepped into their home, I was immediately transported back to my grandma Shirley's home from my childhood. It smelled of something baking in the oven and the sofa beckoned to be curled up on under a soft hand-knit blanket. By our American standards, their home is modest, and their possessions are valued not in dollars, but in sentimental worth. They have lived through an economic collapse in their country and have been robbed on several occasions. Their home isn't bursting with things, yet I believe that is what makes it so special. Rather than filling the four walls with stuff, they have truly filled the air with a spirit of generosity and warmth and true hospitality. The home can breathe and, therefore, it invites others to come in and exhale.

I long to live with such gracious hospitality and commitment to focusing my energy not on buying more and more but on loving my people better and better. Even still, while I often want to sell everything and live as a devout minimalist, we do have five kids, and no matter how many times we purge and organize and repeat the cycle, there will always be *stuff*. It's inevitable. Backpacks, lunch boxes, coats, sporting equipment, shoes. All the necessities of life take up space in our home and can quickly overwhelm and create clutter and disorganization.

We live in a one-hundred-plus-year-old home and storage space is simply not something they planned for a century ago. An intentional drop zone for all our stuff has become an essential component of our home. We have hooks for backpacks and coats and cubbies for shoes and sporting equipment. Now, I wish my children were perfectly trained little humans who appreciate the order a good organizational system provides. But, alas, they're normal kids. And 99 percent of the time, I find coats and backpacks strewn on the floor just below the intended storage hooks.

Yet the small things sometimes teach the most important lessons. So, each day, I remind them to hang a backpack on a hook or place shoes in their cubby instead of leaving them wherever they land as they're hurriedly kicked off on the way inside the house. Or to hang up a shirt and place dirty clothes *inside* a hamper instead of *beside* it. These small things lead to the big things as they grow. Someday, I hope they'll understand that it was never about a tidy mudroom or a stingy momma who wouldn't let them buy a newer, cooler pair of shoes. It has always been about learning responsibility, caring for our belongings, and being grateful for what we have.

Intention

SHEDDING THE OUTSIDE WORLD

Our Drop Zone

I DIDN'T THINK a storage area for each of our kids, just off the door we all use to come in from outside, would work. But I have to give credit for our drop zone to Jenny. It is one space—a little six-foot-by-eight-foot area—with built-in cubbies, places to hang their bags, and places for their shoes, their coats, and their books. Although we take pictures when our drop zone looks perfect, the moment our kids come home from school they've trashed it again. It's the same every day: They drop all their stuff on the floor, right in the drop zone. They grab a snack, then head to the table to do their homework. Once that homework is done, sometimes stuff gets hung up. Sometimes it stays right on the floor in the drop zone until the next day of school, but at least it's all in that one small space. At 7:30 A.M., we are never frantically trying to find stuff while hearing: "Where's my homework?," "Where's my book?," "Where's my bag?," "Where are my shoes?" They're all in our one drop zone. Although it doesn't always look tidy, it's a very real place of organization for our kids, where they can find the things they need every day.

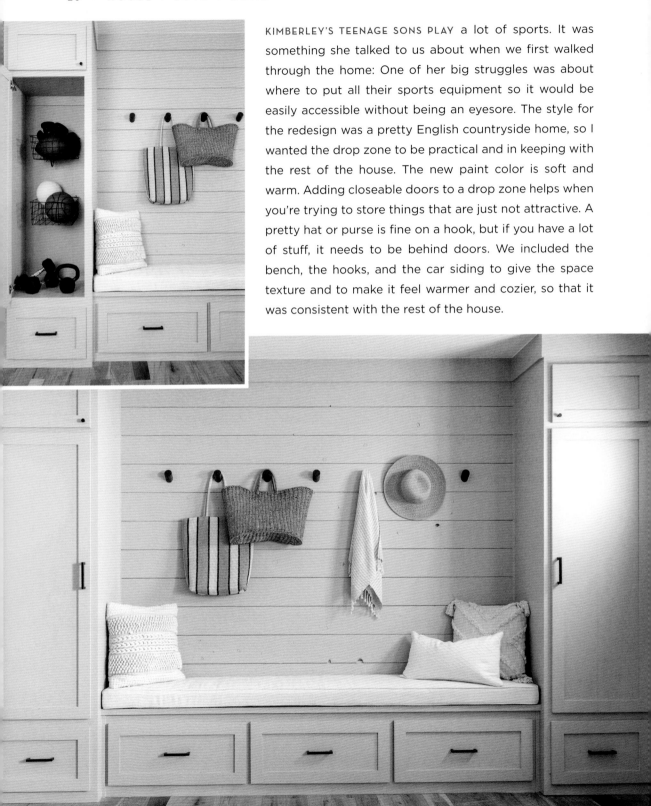

KIMBERLEY'S TEENAGE SONS PLAY a lot of sports. It was something she talked to us about when we first walked through the home: One of her big struggles was about where to put all their sports equipment so it would be easily accessible without being an eyesore. The style for the redesign was a pretty English countryside home, so I wanted the drop zone to be practical and in keeping with the rest of the house. The new paint color is soft and warm. Adding closeable doors to a drop zone helps when you're trying to store things that are just not attractive. A pretty hat or purse is fine on a hook, but if you have a lot of stuff, it needs to be behind doors. We included the bench, the hooks, and the car siding to give the space texture and to make it feel warmer and cozier, so that it was consistent with the rest of the house.

Jenny's Tip

STORAGE BASKETS OF ALL SIZES

I love doors and drawers for storing things, particularly in an entryway, but if you don't have the space for a closet, table, cabinet, or drop zone, a selection of baskets of different sizes— small enough for keys, or big enough for winter scarves, hats, and gloves— can be an easy, attractive solution.

Dave's Corner

BUILDING A BASIC DROP ZONE

I'm going to lay out the steps to build a basic beadboard-backed raised-panel drop zone with two cubbies for storage, a seating area, and hooks for hanging. It's pretty straightforward, and with the right preparation, it can be a good project for a weekend morning. You can make it really simple with just the storage cubbies and hooks or add three boards of housing if you want a more enclosed version. The specs below assume the ceiling of your drop zone is a standard eight feet or higher.

MATERIALS

All-purpose wood glue

One 4 foot x 8 foot sheet of ¼-inch beadboard

18-gauge finish trim nails

Nail gun or hammer

One 4 foot x 8 foot sheet of ¾-inch plywood

One 4 foot x 16 inch sheet of ¾-inch plywood

One 1 inch x 4 inch x 4 foot pine strip

Level

Tape measure

Sandpaper

3 hooks with 2- or 3-hole screw mounts

Stain, varnish, or paint

Painting equipment

1. Set the bottom of the beadboard sheet flush to the floor. If there is a baseboard, cut out a section the length of the beadboard. I start by gluing it to the wall—then I can build everything out in front of it. Nail the corners to the wall. This will be all the backing you need.

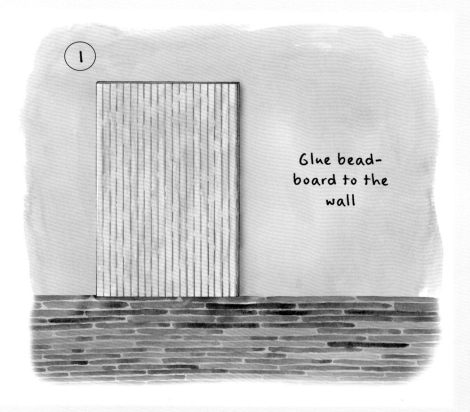

Glue bead-
board to the
wall

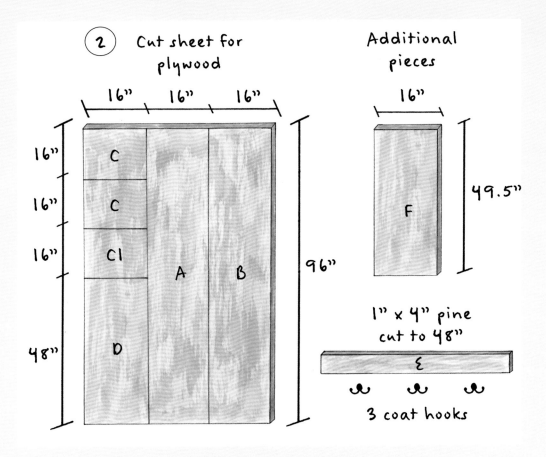

2. Cut (or ask your local lumber seller to cut) your 4 foot x 8 foot plywood piece into:

    a.   Three 8 foot x 16 inch pieces—two of these pieces will be the sides of your housing (A and B) if you are building a contained drop zone.

    b.   Three 16 inch x 16 inch pieces (C, C, C1), using the third 8 foot x 16 inch piece.

The remaining 4 foot x 16 inch piece will be the bench top (D) for the cubbies; 16 inches is a good height for storage and a good width for a seat.

If you are making the enclosed version, you'll need an additional 49½ inch x 16 inch piece of plywood for the top of the housing (F).

3. Glue then nail the narrow side of one of the C pieces to the edge of D. Glue the second C piece to the opposite end of D.

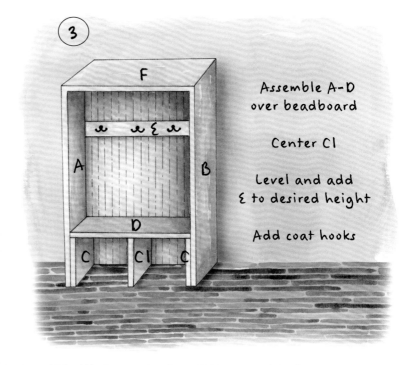

Assemble A–D over beadboard

Center C1

Level and add ξ to desired height

Add coat hooks

4. Glue and nail C1 to the middle of the baseboard, equidistant from the edges of the beadboard.

5. Glue and nail the open rectangular box (D, C, C) to the beadboard and to C1. Once attached, the seating bench will be about 18 inches tall, the height of a standard dining or kitchen chair. You'll now also have two cubbyholes.

6. Use the level to position the pine strip at the height where you'll want to hang your hooks. If the hooks are for kids, make sure to select an appropriate height.

7. Measure the hook placements so that they are equidistant from the edges of the beadboard and one another. Screw hooks into the pine strip. Most hooks come with screws long enough to screw into the pine strip and beadboard. For added anchoring, buy longer screws, which can be screwed into the strip, beadboard, and wall.

8. Sand any sharp corners and edges.

9. Stain, varnish, paint, or keep with plain finish.

BUILDING A CONTAINED DROP ZONE

Glue and nail pieces A, B, and F to the wall and to one another. Position flush to the outside edges of the beadboard.

MY SISTER ANGIE AND I grew up in Florida. Her husband, Rob, moved to Florida when he was in fifth grade. So they've both spent a lot of their lives near the beach. They later lived in Hawaii for nine years, where going to the beach was a big part of their family life: They loved being near the ocean and their sons loved to surf. To honor this part of their lives, Rob requested a fish tank as a surprise for Angie in their new home when they moved to Benton-ville. We wanted a bold moment right when anyone walked through the front door, so we chose a 1,000-gallon aquarium. Our kids were involved in the surprise and helped pick out some of the fish for their cousins as a housewarming gift.

Not only is the aquarium something people talk about as soon as they come into the house, but people who drive by literally slow down to look and ask: What in the world is that thing? It is eye-catching, beautiful, mesmerizing, and ever-changing. Angie and Rob spend each morning having coffee while watching the fish. It's a soothing, peaceful moment at the start of their day.

Jenny's Tip

**YOUR PERSONAL STORY DOESN'T NEED
TO BE A 1,000-GALLON AQUARIUM,
BUT IT CAN BE AS EVER-CHANGING**

The entry area or hallway is a visitor's first experience of your home. It's your chance to introduce the story of who you are and what is important to you. Part of your story might be told through a gallery wall of family photos, a treasured object from a memorable trip, or a favorite piece of art. It can be anything unique to you that can serve as a conversation starter and statement piece for your guests. Having an area near your front door where you can display cherished objects, photos, heirlooms, artwork, or souvenirs can be a way to tell your—and your family's—story. Our stories aren't static. Like my sister's aquarium, they can be ever-changing. Consider swapping out items now and then to keep your story fresh and evolving.

TRANSFORMATIONAL TIP *Hallway Lighting & Flooring Options*

This entry hallway was originally very dark, with no natural light, limited over-head lighting, and dark hardwood floors. To brighten the hallway and create a welcoming entrance to the home, we installed an antique wooden front door with glass in order to bring in natural light and add warmth. We also removed the drop ceiling to expose the original ten-foot ceilings and incorporated period-appropriate overhead sconces and wooden beams to draw the eye upward. The original floors were refinished and sealed with a natural epoxy to brighten the space from the ground up. Lighter wood floors, natural lighting, and ample over-head lighting are key components to brightening up a tight space.

THE BREWER FAMILY HAS lived in their home for multiple generations. It was built by the current owner's great-grandparents in 1926 and holds almost a century of memories. In order to honor the rich history of this family home upon entering, I gathered the amazing pieces that the Brewers had saved over the years and created a gallery wall in the hallway. The gallery wall features photos and everyday documents that have become treasured family keepsakes, such as local newspaper clippings from the 1930s, an original schematic of the house, and a water bill from the 1940s for the amount of three dollars. Now the moment anyone enters this home, they are greeted with the stories and heritage of this special place and family.

Jenny's Tip

PHOTO LEDGES IN HIGH-TRAFFIC AREAS

The side entrance of our home is a high-traffic area, as it leads to the garage and back patio. Because there is constant activity in this small space, I wanted to create a display of family photos and kids' artwork without the use of a gallery wall. As a solution, I had Dave build photo ledges so that I could stack frames along the wall. If I had hung the photos, they would have gotten knocked into and rarely hung straight. The photo ledge allows me to stack framed memorabilia without worrying about them falling or looking askew.

CHAPTER 3

GATHERING

EATING SPACES

—

*School Lunches &
Dinner Times*

WHEN I WAS TWELVE years old, our Central Florida school board decided to rezone our district. Because I lived on the east side of Lake Underhill Drive, I was moved into the new zoning area and had to leave my close-knit group of childhood friends to attend seventh grade at a new middle school. These friendships had been formed on the preschool playground and nurtured throughout my elementary school years. I panicked at the thought of leaving my familiar world and going somewhere new, alone.

The defining moment of that first day happened at the lunch hour. As I walked away from the lunch line, tray in hand, scanning the cafeteria for an empty seat, I silently tried to will someone—anyone—to look up and make eye contact with me. Thankfully, a girl with dark, curly hair and a warm smile saw the desperate look in my eyes and waved me over. Relief washed over me as I placed my tray on her table and sat awkwardly in the plastic chair. She introduced herself as Elise and we immediately hit it off and started comparing class schedules. Elise and I quickly became dear friends, and we were inseparable during the next two years. When it was time to go to high school, we were in separate school zones, and I settled back in with my childhood friends at Colonial High while Elise was across town at University High. Even though we no longer saw each other every day, we remained close friends and, four years later, attended the same college. We became college roommates and we were bridesmaids in each other's weddings. All the shared memories and laughter and encouragement spanning years of friendship are rooted in that single moment of kindness when Elise reached out to invite me over to her table on my first lonely day at a new school.

There is something about sitting at a table and sharing a meal that evokes a sense of belonging like nowhere else can. It's the place where hospitality is tangibly offered and where lines of division become blurred. For my seventh-grade self, that invitation to sit was also an invitation for a new friendship that would span a lifetime. At the time, I was simply relieved not to be singled out by sitting alone. I had no way of knowing how deeply this new person would impact my life or how this lesson of generosity and the importance of a welcoming spirit would stay with me all these years later.

The idea of a shared table, a place where everyone can have a seat, has remained a powerful concept to me. When we remodeled our kitchen a few years ago,

I knew I wanted the dining table to be the focal point because I believe it represents so much more than just a place to sit and eat. The table is sacred. It is a place set aside specifically for nourishing our bodies, and often our souls as well. When we sit around the table and pass salad bowls or warm bread, we are carving out a moment to silence the outside noise of the world. We are letting our racing minds and ragged bodies be still and accept nourishment.

When we reconfigured our kitchen and dining areas, I decided to take a bold step and remove the central island. This allowed us to extend the kitchen cabinetry into the former dining nook and place a large dining table smack in the center of it all. Granted, this is counterintuitive to how most contemporary kitchens are designed. Most families we work with ask for a large kitchen island and a separate dining space. But our old home has very limited square footage and we had to make a choice in order to use the space well: either a large island or a dining table—we couldn't fit both. So we got creative, broke the traditional "kitchen design" mold, and went for it.

Dave built a beautiful, long white maple table that truly is the workhorse of our home. It serves as the central hub and gathering place for our family and guests. Our kids congregate at this table for homework, crafts, and meals. We knead bread and mix cupcakes here. We check emails here. We play board games around the table. It's where life happens. This table tells our family's story in tangible ways: The crayon marks, the stray crumbs, and the nicks in the wood all speak of the life that happens here and the memories being formed around this table.

At our dinner table each evening, we play the question game. We take turns

asking questions and choosing someone to answer. Sometimes, the questions are silly: *Would you rather live in a treehouse, a boat, or an igloo?* When it's my turn to answer, I say, *Definitely not a treehouse because I'm afraid of heights and I'd probably roll out in my sleep and break a leg. But I get seasick and would be miserable on a boat. So I'll go with an igloo, but I'd have to install central heat and indoor plumbing.* Nate immediately debates that heat and indoor plumbing would be scientifically impossible inside

an igloo and Ben tries to convince me to change my answer to a boat, claiming I would eventually get my sea legs. Charlotte declares she'll live with me in the igloo if she can have a pet penguin. Sylvie gets on board with Char's idea and asks for a pet polar bear, which then causes two-year-old Luke to jump up on the table and roar like a bear while Dave pretends to be a bear hunter. Our table erupts in giggles.

One of my favorite questions is very simple: *What is one thing you love about the person sitting to your left?* The answers are honest and gentle: *You are working to get your grades up, which is awesome,* or *I love how sweet you are,* or *I love how you love our animals and take good care of them.*

As I watch the recipient of the affirming words, I witness the subtle shift in their eyes as they take in the truths spoken about them. Their eyes always begin downcast and uncomfortable, because waiting to hear what someone you love thinks of you is a vulnerable position to be in. Then, they eventually look up and directly at the person speaking about them. That's when I see it. Their eyes have changed. They are no longer nervous and shy; instead they have become bright and bold. This is exactly what the table is for: a place to expose our most honest selves and, in return, receive the gift of being cared for in loving and meaningful ways.

The table is also magical in the way that it can foster deep and authentic community. My parents recently made the move from Florida to our little northwest corner of Arkansas and my older sister, Angie, and her family also live in town. To have my family close by has been the sweetest, most unexpected gift. Over the years, our tradition of a Sunday friends' dinner has shifted as kids have grown and commitments have changed. These days, Sunday dinner includes our extended families. Dave's family is all local, and when we host Sunday night dinners in our modest-sized home, it is full to the brim. When our entire family is here, there are twenty-six of us gathered around our dining table and even more when friends join the meal. Often we overflow out onto the back porch table. There's nothing that energizes my spirit or fuels my soul more than the sound of chairs scraping on the floor as they are rearranged to make room for another person.

I love the dance that occurs when everyone arrives for Sunday dinner. The kitchen teems with life as our kids run in from outside to greet our guests and cousins pair up and run back out again. There is a flurry of activity and lighthearted chatter as the adults work around one another, reaching for plates, cutting vegetables, or pouring drinks.

The table overflows with platters and sacks of food and bottles of wine as each arrival brings something to add to the meal. In the winter months, there is always a large crock of soup simmering on the stove, red wine decanted and ready to be poured into wide-rimmed glasses. At the first hint of spring, we open windows, allowing a soft breeze to clear out the stale winter air. We turn up music, make heaping salads with fresh-picked vegetables, and set out charcuterie boards laden with sharp cheeses and sweet fruits.

Some nights find us around the table, candles burned low, empty plates not yet cleared, sharing stories that leave us doubled up in laughter. Some nights, we sit quietly as someone shares their heartache or fear. The kids love when my mom tells stories about the childhood antics of my siblings and me.

Sometimes, everyone leaves early and we tuck the kids into bed on time. Often, we stay up too late laughing and storytelling and lament the lack of sleep the next day. Those nights around our table have only reinforced the importance of family and deep connections forged over a shared meal. When this world feels turned upside down and the clatter is deafening, I've learned it's best to step away from the clamor, open up the door, and fill every seat at the table.

JAY AND LAURA D'SPAIN'S KITCHEN eating area had a bay window next to it that provided light, but the space itself wasn't optimized for seating and felt cramped. We added a built-in bench to the window to square off the angles and create additional seating. Wood flooring across the kitchen and breakfast nook seamlessly tied the two spaces together. As a nod to the important people and events in Jay's and Laura's lives, Dave reworked a photo memory board using a large piece of flat magnetic steel in order to echo design details of the steel kitchen island. The space is now better utilized and the board on the wall tells their family's story in a beautiful, modern way.

Jenny's Tip

SPACE-SAVING SOLUTIONS FOR EATING AREAS

In a tight space, I like to incorporate a built-in banquette. This allows the table to move closer to the wall and optimizes the overall footprint of the space. I also like to incorporate bench seating in a tight dining space, since the bench can tuck all the way under the table when people aren't sitting at it. It's also a great solution for young kids—a lot of little kids can fit on a bench in a pinch. When using a bench at a table, I like to balance the hard material with softer options like upholstered chairs or caned seating for texture. I also like to have extra dining chairs on hand that can be pulled out for dinner, hidden as useful pieces of furniture in other places around the house—like a chair that holds towels in the bathroom or an extra set of chairs on the patio. I never want a family to lack for places to offer hospitality, especially when it comes to plenty of seating for a meal.

SINGLE DAD STAN ZYLOWSKI co-parents his two sons with their mom, so he wanted to ensure his boys had two homes rather than "home" and "Dad's house." He wanted to create a home for them where they could embrace and enjoy all the things they love to do together now, including their gaming-and-hosting-friends lifestyle. The house had no dining area, which was something Stan specifically asked for, so we transformed the unused entry and reworked the footprint of the room to create a dining space. Taking an idea from the owner's (and his sons') love of baseball, Dave built a custom banquette of ash wood, a low-key nod to the wood used to make baseball bats, and the faux leather cushions were inspired by the supple texture and appearance of a worn baseball glove. The new dining table, lighting, paint, and wood flooring create a cozy entry area, for dining and for hanging—right off the bat.

Dave

The Everything Table

BEFORE WE REMODELED our home, we had a small kitchen, a small island, and a small dining room table. The challenge was figuring out how to create a big wide-open kitchen with an island and still have a dining room table. In this small farmhouse we couldn't make it work; there wasn't room. So Jenny said, "I know this is counter to what everyone says to do, but what if we scrap the island, and our kitchen is a giant table, which becomes the island and where we do Life?" It's worked out really well. Jenny wanted a light maple wood, something that was durable but would scratch, show wear, show time, and show that life has been experienced around it. I built this table with the intention for it to be as big as it could possibly be. In making it that big, we had to scrap the chairs on the back side of it and built a bench that everyone could slide onto. Everything that we do is centered around this table. It's the centerpiece of our whole main floor. We've now used this idea in several homes we've remodeled in recent years.

THE LENNARD FAMILY loves to host people in their home. They've taken in foreign-exchange students and have kept an open door for family and friends. With no space in

the floor plan for a separate dining room, the owners welcomed the idea of creating an area in their kitchen where they could share meals with loved ones and their steady stream of guests. Instead of an island, they opted for an eight-foot-long oak table like the one Dave and I have in our own kitchen. Dave built this beautiful table to serve as their main gathering place.

Intention

SHARING OUR STORIES & SHARING OURSELVES

THE BEAUTY OF THIS REMODEL was that we had an open canvas to work with. Once we established what spaces we needed to plan for, we were able to define where walls would be framed in, and then we were able to fill those spaces. We knew we needed to create a living room, kitchen, and dining room that would flow into one another but still be distinctive areas. We worked with the owners—one of whom was originally from NYC—to give the space

modern and industrial touches that echoed a loft-like space from his home city. Because the multiuse space has muted colors and industrial features throughout, I added a pop of light and bold color by asking an artist friend of one of the owners to paint a bright floral mural. The mural adds contrast to the rest of the modern industrial space and is a statement piece that helps make the dining area unique.

TRANSFORMATIONAL TIP *Defining Dining Room Spaces*

Often, dining areas are incorporated into an open floor plan, so a challenge can arise when trying to create a dining space that feels cozy and warm despite being connected to the larger space. Of course, the shape of the table helps to define the area and while I most often use rectangular tables, for the right space, a round table can be effective for drawing people together and creating opportunities for conversation and sharing. When appropriate, a large rug beneath the dining table that extends a few feet beyond its edge can help to keep things feeling contained and separate. The most effective way to define a dining space and create a focal point is through well-thought-out lighting placement. There are multiple options—wall sconces, pendant lighting, recessed can lights, a chandelier—the key being that the light is cast in directions and angles that highlight the dining table and the area around it.

THIS DINING ROOM REFLECTS the late 1800s time period when the home was built. We wanted the small
room to feel larger, which we accomplished in a cou-
ple of ways. First, new French doors leading out to the garden brought in natural light; and
second, we removed the drop ceiling to expose the floor joists above and create more height.
The ceiling beams are original and add warmth and dimension to the room. The two-light
chandelier was handmade in a vintage style that matches the era of the home. To finish off
the space, Dave built an oval dining table out of black walnut that looks like an antique and
is slightly formal to coordinate with the elevated feel of this room.

THE COUGHLINS ENJOY entertaining friends and family, and bought this house to host guests at the lake. We wanted to create an airy space with an expansive view of the water, so we opened up the wall separating the kitchen and dining area and installed massive windows. A striking, finely shaped metal chandelier on a dimmer casts a cozy cloud of light as evening arrives, with the area rug helping to make the open space feel intimate. We also installed wood flooring and wood paneling on the ceiling for texture and visual interest.

Jenny's Tip

ENCOURAGING SHARING & CONNECTION
THROUGH LIGHTING DECISIONS

While the placement of lighting is important for defining the actual space of the seating and dining area, the quality of the light really sets the mood for the room. To encourage sharing stories around the table, which is a very vulnerable thing to do, you need a place that feels warm, where people feel comfortable and connected to the people they are sitting with. A softly lit chandelier during dinner or tabletop candles help create a magical glow. Installing a dimmer is a simple option and one of the quickest ways to help set the mood. The choice of bulbs can play a big role—it's important to consider wattage, warmth, and light spectrum when installing bulbs in any space.

Dave's Corner

BULB CHOICES

When working to create a cozy space through overhead lighting, you need to consider light quality. There is a basic K (Kelvin) rating system on light bulbs. You can choose light quality from 1,000K to 5,000K: 1,000 is similar to an Edison bulb and 5,000 is similar to a hospital surgical theater. We usually choose between 2,700 and 3,000K for the optimal light quality, and we try to use all LED dimmable bulbs. They give off a nice warm light that's not too yellow or too stark white.

CHAPTER 4

NOURISHING

KITCHENS & COOKING SPACES

—

*Great-Grandma Thelma,
Grandma Marrs & Dr. Laure*

MY PARENTS MET IN the fifth grade, after my dad's family moved from Chicago to Orlando and his parents fortuitously bought a house two streets over from my mom's childhood home. As my dad settled into the area, he became fast friends with the small group of neighborhood kids, which included my mom and her siblings. They all spent their summer afternoons hanging around the baseball field at the end of the street, playing pickup games and, inevitably, my dad would chase my mom home afterward. She lightheartedly claims she was unamused by his antics. Still, he eventually won her over and they began dating in high school, marrying right after graduation. Because my grandfather, whom I called Papa, would only approve of the marriage if my dad had a job, he was hired to work in the family business: Darland Bakery. Papa's mom, Thelma Darland, started the bakery out of her home kitchen in 1951, and by the time my parents married in 1975, Papa had taken over what had developed into a wholesale bakery business that moved out of Thelma's kitchen and into a large warehouse and office building located near downtown Orlando on South Street. My mom became the bakery bookkeeper, and my dad was assigned the task of managing operational

logistics in what we all knew as "the back of the bakery." "The back" housed all the actual baking equipment, and my dad was in charge of everything from ordering ingredients to developing recipes and executing all of the actual day-to-day baking.

While I never had a chance to meet Great-Grandma Thelma Darland, her baking legacy lived on in our family. My dad was always inventing new recipes, and my siblings and I happily volunteered to be his taste-testers. My parents lived and breathed that small family bakery, and my childhood memories are inextricably tied to the flavor of flaky pie crusts filled with sugary pecans and of warm berry crumble muffins slathered in butter. My three siblings and I spent countless summer days folding muffin boxes in the bakery warehouse, where we earned one penny per box. Our earnings were particularly slim in the summer of 1988, as we were inspired to create an Olympian-approved obstacle course out of 100-pound bags of flour and metal bakery racks. We would excitedly run to the warehouse in the morning, hoping to beat the previous day's record time. Our parents had no idea we were in there swinging from pallet lifts and climbing over precariously stacked buckets of walnuts instead of folding boxes.

Our house was never without an abundance of baked goods that my parents would bring home after work, and my friends loved to gather in my kitchen, gobbling up rich Danishes drizzled in decadent frosting as an afterschool snack. To this day, whenever I catch a whiff of a pie bubbling in the oven, I'm immediately taken back to that beloved building on South Street. A childhood spent in a bakery is just about as sweet as they come, and I will forever be a dessert person.

Never did I display my devotion to

baked goods more than when I was pregnant with the twins. For many months, Dave and Grandma Marrs could be found in our kitchen, baking her deliciously simple four-ingredient peanut butter cookies, which I consumed at an astronomical rate. I craved those peanut butter cookies throughout the day and at all hours of the night. Grandma taught me that they were best frozen, so she would stack them in neat layers in our freezer, and I would smile each time I opened the freezer to find the tasty treats. I'd dip the frozen cookie in ice-cold milk, take a bite, and let out a deep sigh of satisfaction. Crumbs would fall onto my round belly, and I'd scoop them up and pop them into my mouth. I briefly toyed with the idea that I should cut back on the cookie calories, but I justified my consumption because I was growing two humans and this was my first and long-fought-for pregnancy, so I gave myself a pass to eat whatever I wanted.

When I was twenty-nine weeks along, I unexpectedly went into preterm labor and, after twelve hours of medical intervention to prevent a premature delivery, I was airlifted to Little Rock because our local hospital's NICU wasn't equipped to care for twenty-nine-week-old preemies. As the helicopter raced through the night sky, Dave held my trembling hand while hot tears streamed down my cheeks. Upon arrival at the University of Arkansas for Medical Sciences, we were given every worst-case scenario from the medical team and were told the boys would certainly be born within the next twenty-four hours. We absorbed their words in silence. Dave assured me everything would be okay and then quietly left the room to regain his composure in the hall. He came back after several minutes, eyes red-rimmed but otherwise I was convinced he believed the words he spoke to me: *It's going to be okay.* We huddled together on the hospital bed and prayed and cried and begged God for another hour for the boys to grow in utero. And then, when one hour passed, we exhaled briefly and started praying for another hour. Every single hour that passed was a small miracle.

Meanwhile, both of our families drove to the hospital to be with us. Dave's family arrived first, and his parents were allowed to see us. Against all odds, twenty-four hours turned into thirty-six and then into forty-eight. After three days, I was finally allowed to eat a cracker and sip on orange juice, and I declared it the finest meal I had ever eaten.

I went on to stay on strict bed rest in the hospital for the next four weeks. Dave slept on the uncomfortable sleeper sofa each night and would pace the halls of the hospital each day when he was restless. Our families visited weekly, and I will never forget Grandma Marrs arriving one afternoon with a tin packed full of her peanut butter cookies. She made sure to get me a little carton of milk from the cafeteria and simply sat on the edge of my bed while I ate one. I don't know if it was the thousand little miracles I had seen transpire over the course of the previous weeks or the sheer relief that the boys were still safely in utero or the utter kindness and thoughtfulness she had shown by baking those cookies and then hand-delivering them four hours away from home at ninety years old, but that cookie tasted divine.

The boys were born on May 29, 2010, exactly four weeks after that terrifying helicopter ride through the Arkansas night sky. We were able to come back to Northwest Arkansas and live together in our local hospital for the next four weeks as the boys gained strength in the NICU. On the long-awaited day when we were finally released, Dave carefully drove home while I sat in the back of the car, squeezed between the two car seats. I marveled at these miraculous little guys and whispered prayers of gratitude for their fighting spirits. After eight weeks of living in a hospital, we arrived home to find a large banner over the garage and entered a sparkling-clean kitchen with flowers and balloons covering the expanse of our countertops. I crossed the room to place the boys' stash of frozen milk in the freezer and smiled contentedly as I discovered that Grandma had filled a shelf with neatly stacked bags of her cookies: the perfect homecoming gift.

Two years later, I befriended Laure Nakweti who, like Grandma Marrs, lovingly serves through the tangible gift of food. Dr. Laure is a Congolese doctor and mother of six, to whom I was introduced by a mutual friend at the start of our family's adoption journey. She lives close to the orphanage where our daughter Sylvie was living at the time, and she agreed to bring a warm meal and check in on Sylvie and the other children there. Upon hearing from Dr. Laure after her first visit, I knew that the orphanage—a small compound with two concrete buildings framing a dirt courtyard in the center—was no place for a child. There was no grass for playing, only coarse dirt, which stained the soles of their bare feet and created a dusty film over every surface. They slept on concrete floors and a handful of holes in the ground served as a restroom for the fifty-four children there. Food was scarce and most days the children each received only one small helping of fufu. Fufu is a traditional Congolese side dish made from water and corn flour that fills bellies and can be made inexpensively. It's typically served with stew, chicken, or vegetables, but these additional items were an extravagance the orphanage couldn't afford. The children there were visibly malnourished.

When Dr. Laure arrived with armfuls of food, she was greeted with cheers and shrieks of joy.

Six months later, Dr. Laure welcomed Sylvie into her home as a foster child and lovingly ensured that she was being cared for and fed daily. She continued her monthly food deliveries to the orphanage, supported by the generosity of our friends and family here in the States. Sylvie lived under Dr. Laure's roof for thirteen months as we waited helplessly on the other side of the globe, completing infinite mounds of paperwork and battling government red tape and bureaucratic procedures.

I was in the regular habit of waking in the night to check my email, knowing that news coming out of the Democratic Republic of the Congo would arrive to me in the very early morning hours. On July 7, 2014, at 4:18 A.M., I received the best email of my life from the State Department in Kinshasa:

> *Dear Marrs Family,*
>
> *We are very happy to inform you that the DGM has told us that Sylvie's exit permit will be ready for pick-up today at noon. Please let us know if you plan on picking it up yourselves while you are in country or whether your in-country representative will be picking it up.*
>
> *Thanks, Saskia*

I screamed and reached over to wake Dave to relay the news. His side of the bed was empty, ruffled sheets revealing a restless night. I ran to the kitchen, where I found him sitting at the table reading. Time felt suspended as I raced toward him. I noticed the steam rising from his coffee mug and watched as his expression shifted from a greeting to concern as he saw how visibly shaken I was. My heart racing, my voice quavering, I read him the email and then collapsed into his arms in a heap of sobs.

We took a breath and immediately called Dr. Laure. Collectively, we agreed it would be wise for her to bring Sylvie to us. Sylvie knew she was safe with Dr. Laure and while Sylvie had met us during our visits there and we talked regularly on video calls, the process of leaving everything and everyone she'd ever known would be traumatizing for her two-year-old mind to process. Dave booked flights for Sylvie and Dr. Laure to leave Kinshasa the following day and begin their long journey over the sea.

I tracked the flights and kept in communication with Dr. Laure throughout their travels. However, when my flight tracker showed they had arrived in Chicago, she didn't call for more than two hours and I knew something was wrong. I tried calling but it went straight to voicemail each time. I started to worry.

Mercifully, my phone finally rang and her name appeared on the screen. I learned that they had been detained in customs because Dr. Laure had packed fish and vegetables in her luggage in order to cook a traditional Congolese meal for us at our home during her stay.

Once the confusion was resolved and they boarded their connecting flight, we held our breath in anticipation of the plane finally—after 602 days of waiting—touching down in our little regional airport here at home. Words can never truly explain the relief, the immense gratitude, and the sheer emotional exhaustion we experienced that afternoon at Gate 9B when I ran to greet Dr. Laure and then held my daughter in my arms for the first time on U.S. soil, knowing I would never have to leave her again.

Later that week, Dr. Laure insisted on cooking for us, and I will always cherish the memory of our lighthearted chatter and comfortable silence as we stood together in my kitchen. We chopped vegetables side by side, Sylvie sitting on a little stool between us, giggling and speaking an adorable combination of toddler gibberish, French, and broken English. Dr. Laure patiently described the process of making fufu to me as she moved through the familiar motions. Music softly played in the background, and the open windows carried in the breeze along with the melody of laughter from Dave and the boys as they played outside in the yard. Eight-week-old Charlotte slept peacefully in the swing at my feet. While it appeared to be an ordinary moment of a meal being prepared among friends, it was so much more. It was a celebration. That day, our kitchen was infused with both the delicious spicy smells of Congolese cooking and a palpable, unmistakable joy.

GRANDMA MARRS'S PEANUT BUTTER COOKIES

1 cup peanut butter
1 cup sugar
1 egg
1 teaspoon baking soda

Preheat oven to 350°F.

Mix all the ingredients together in a medium bowl.

Roll the dough into little balls, slightly larger than a teaspoon, and place on the sheet about 2 inches apart.

Smash each ball with the bottom of a glass dipped in sugar. Repeat with more sugar.

Press lines in a crisscross pattern into the dough with the back of a fork.

Bake for about 10 minutes, until cookies are slightly brown along edges. Transfer to a wire rack to cool completely.

THIS KITCHEN IS OPEN and spacious, with plenty of room for a large island and a dining table. The wall of floor-to-ceiling pantry cabinets creates plenty of storage (vital in a historic home) and looks gorgeous, with an English-country charm. It was important to me and the owner, Ashley, that we incorporate vintage pieces, so I added a pair of oversized vintage schoolhouse pendant lights above the island, as well as a set of beautiful matching stained-glass windows, found at a local antiques shop, on either side of the range, which added character to the new, modern windows. The overall look and feel I wanted for this kitchen was a timeless, functional, and beautiful space that was period-appropriate but still had all of the necessary modern amenities.

WHEN WE WERE REMODEL-
ING my sister's home, a
beautiful and functional
kitchen was the top priority
for her family. As a professional chef, my brother-in-
law wanted a proper chef's
kitchen. Not to mention
that we have a large family
and he and my sister love
to host Sunday family dinners, so the open concept
and an extra-large island
with ample seating were a
must for entertaining. The
new kitchen has plenty of
counter space for prep, an
abundance of cabinet storage, a gorgeous 60-inch
Italian range, and four wall
ovens. The quarter-sawed

white oak cabinetry
creates a modern,
yet warm and invit-
ing overall aesthetic.

THIS MODERN INDUSTRIAL KITCHEN is bold without feeling cold and stark. I kept this design open—simple, yet practical. It's perfect for allowing large groups to gather, but not so big that it threw off the proportions of the larger open space within which the kitchen is housed. As a nod to the owner's love for antique brick, I added a wall of brick veneer to give the illusion that this kitchen is in a former warehouse. To continue the modern lines and let in extra light, we added upper windows that stretch the width of the cabinetry.

Color

KATHLEEN, THE OWNER OF this home, wanted a unique and bold kitchen. She told me to go either all black or all white. When we reviewed Kathleen's images of kitchens she loved, I saw a clear trend toward all black. I absolutely adore how sophisticated and stunning the kitchen turned out. Custom cabinets and countertops, modern hardware, brass fixtures, a big island, and a uniform shade of black all over resulted in a gorgeous showstopper of a kitchen. I love the black tiles behind the range and the woven hanging light fixtures that infuse a casual vibe and a contrasting texture into this sharp, modern kitchen.

TRANSFORMATIONAL TIP *Color*

A bold color for a kitchen is not for everyone. I know that Dave would never agree to a bold cabinet color in our own kitchen—or if he did agree it would take a lot of persuading. When we did the black kitchen shown here, Dave was concerned it would be too dark, but in the end, he agreed that it turned out beautifully. As you consider your own kitchen color scheme, return to the idea of how you want the space to make you and others feel. Dark colors are eye-catching and add drama. Often in a small space, a dark color can work very well, creating a sophisticated, yet cozy atmosphere. A lighter color makes a kitchen feel bright and airy. Personally, I prefer muted neutral tones rather than stark white to obtain the freshness of a light kitchen while maintaining charm and character. Wood cabinetry or shelving adds instant warmth. Regardless of color choice, I always use a low-sheen oil-based paint for easy cleanup. For wood cabinets, I always seal with a water-based clear coat rather than oil-based, which will cause the wood to look yellow.

GAYATRI, THE OWNER OF this kitchen, loves vibrant colors. Her old kitchen had a poster in vivid pinks, yellows, and blues that read, "This kitchen is made for dancing," which became the inspiration for the remodel. I wanted the new kitchen to be infused with color, pattern, and enough space to dance. Because her favorite color is pink, I chose a bold pink range as the main focal point. The backsplash has a subtle pattern and brings in a touch of yellow that feels like sunshine. We reoriented the kitchen to create enough space around the new island. It's now a joyful space perfect for dancing.

THIS CABIN IS tucked away in the woods, and I wanted the new kitchen to reflect the lush forest outside. To infuse warmth, we installed natural wood paneling and painted the new cabinets a rich green. This family loves homemade pizza nights and a new indoor pizza oven, surrounded by natural stone, is a beautiful, functional, and really fun focal point. A full wall of cabinetry provides ample storage, with closed doors to hide away small appliances and clutter.

JENNY'S FAVORITE PAINT COLORS

Kitchen

Benjamin Moore
White Dove

Farrow & Ball
Drop Cloth

Benjamin Moore
Revere Pewter

Farrow & Ball
De Nimes

Farrow & Ball
Inchyra Blue

Farrow & Ball
Pigeon

Farrow & Ball
Green Smoke

Farrow & Ball
Treron

Farrow & Ball
Off-Black

Floors

THE OWNERS OF THIS HISTORIC home wanted to retain as many of the original elements as possible. In this case, the original wood floors were in fairly good condition, and we were able to patch a few spots with the same type and size of wood. Because we were able to sand and refinish the original floors, we were able to preserve history, save the homeowners money, and create a beautiful floor throughout their home.

TRANSFORMATIONAL TIP *Flooring Flow*

I personally prefer to use consistent flooring throughout a home to help each space feel cohesive, particularly in an open-concept floor plan. If a kitchen is separate from the rest of the home, it can be an opportunity to incorporate an unexpected floor tile for color and pattern. However, I'd say 99 percent of the time, I incorporate the same wood flooring in a kitchen as I use in the other main spaces of a home to help the rooms flow seamlessly.

WE USED CONCRETE flooring in this kitchen and throughout the surrounding open-plan space to heighten the modern industrial feel that the owners were looking for.

(DAVE: We polished the concrete down to smooth it, and then sealed it. Concrete is just stone, so it is porous; until you seal it, it can be easily stained, so you need to use a stone sealer, the way you would for a countertop or tile and grout.)

THIS BLACK-AND-WHITE-PATTERNED TILE worked well with the white upper shelves and white tiles to balance out the beautiful green of the cabinetry. The kitchen was in a separate space in the back and didn't need to connect to the rest of the house, allowing us to give it its own unique design.

DAVE AND I RECENTLY restored a historic home built in the late 1800s and transformed it into a vacation rental called the Welcome Inn. For this home, I was inspired by the simplicity and beauty of a British cottage kitchen and knew I wanted either brick or an interesting wood flooring in the kitchen. With that in mind, we created this beautiful herringbone pattern that set the tone for the design of the rest of the kitchen.

Jenny's Tip

RUGS & RUNNERS IN THE KITCHEN

I love to use a vintage Turkish runner in a kitchen to add texture and soft, muted color. I prefer to place runners under the sink to add warmth and functional comfort—it provides you a little cushion as you wash the dishes. Another reason I prefer a vintage Turkish runner is because they hold up well in high-traffic areas. If they get dirty, you can easily take them outside to pressure wash and hang to dry.

Shelving

Shelving—Open, Closed & Glass-Fronted

A controversial topic in kitchen design is open shelving. Some people prefer closed cabinetry to prevent open shelves from feeling cluttered or possibly getting messy and dusty. Personally, I love open shelving because it helps me to minimize clutter and provides an opportunity to display the things I love. I keep the beloved dishes Dave and I received as a wedding gift on our open shelves. We use these every day and clean them frequently, so we never have an issue with dusty dishes or glasses.

A balanced kitchen has a combination of cabinetry and shelving to make the space feel thoughtfully designed. Open shelves or glass fronts break up upper cabinetry to prevent a kitchen from feeling too dark and enclosed. Countertop cabinets look beautiful and provide space to hide small appliances. When developing a cabinet plan, it's important to consider how each and every cabinet will be used. And then, get creative and mix in elements such as a small open shelf or a glass-fronted set of cabinets to help the overall beauty and flow of the kitchen layout.

Dave's Corner

BUILDING AN ENCLOSED FLOATING SHELF

Floating shelves are versatile and easy to make. They can be as simple as a plank screwed into the wall to create a great photo ledge in a narrow hallway, like the one we have in our mudroom. Jenny changes family picture frames on it with the seasons. You can use enclosed floating shelves wherever you need shelves strong enough to hold heavy objects, like the shelves we have in our kitchen; they also add a really cool, modern, more finished look.

Here's how to make an enclosed floating shelf:

1. Position and level a two-by-four of your desired length on the wall, then anchor it using screws.

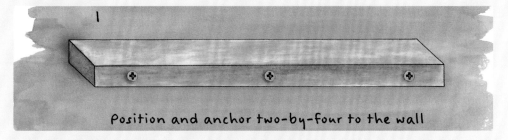

Position and anchor two-by-four to the wall

2. Make a hollow box out of ½-inch or ¾-inch plywood (¾-inch is the same price but stronger) with the same length as your two-by-four, the depth you want for your finished shelf, and a 3-inch height. The box will be open on one of the length sides. We used white oak instead of plywood for our kitchen shelves, but you can choose another wood that gives it the finish you want.

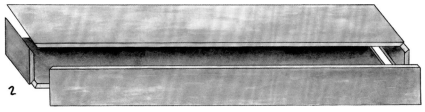

Create a hollow box - bevel edges at a 45-degree angle

3. Slide the box over the two-by-four and secure it to the wall with screws or nails.

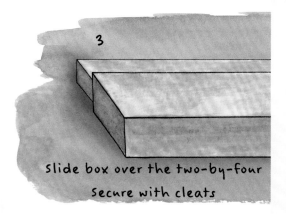

Slide box over the two-by-four
Secure with cleats

Lighting

TRANSFORMATIONAL TIP *Planning Lighting*

Lighting in the kitchen is extremely important. Well-thought-out and versatile lighting is necessary for all the work that goes on in a kitchen and is important for visual focal points.

Natural light is ideal. I truly believe the more natural light in a kitchen, the better. Sometimes you have to forgo cabinet space to add windows, but, in most cases, it is worth it to allow a kitchen to breathe and feel larger.

I prefer having each light fixture on its own switch to serve as functional task lighting. I also like to thoughtfully plan ample overhead can lighting, along with sconces above windows or alongside a range, and appropriately sized pendants above an island.

I LOVE HOW these antique oversized schoolhouse pendants add warmth and vintage charm to the new kitchen in this historic home.

THIS MODERN PENDANT serves as a beautiful statement piece above this oversized island.

THE WOVEN BASKET pendants over the island add texture to this modern lakeside kitchen.

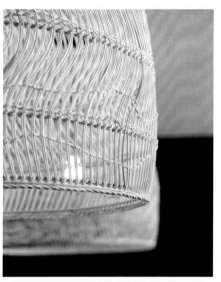

Jenny's Tip

SWAPPING OUT PENDANTS & SCONCES

Sometimes an entire kitchen overhaul is not necessary or feasible, but a fairly simple and highly impactful change can occur by replacing outdated lighting. Lighting is often overlooked yet it can set the tone for an entire kitchen. Adding sconces can feel very thoughtful, as they provide task-centered lighting that can also be beautiful and give the space personality. I love to work with small companies that make handmade lights because they are unique and high quality. Small lighting companies or sites like Etsy are great sources for unique pendants and sconces.

THE OWNER OF THIS house believes the kitchen is the heart of her home and wanted the space to be warm, welcoming, and functional for cooking and baking. Since her double mastectomy, lifting heavy appliances is no longer possible for her, so we added a built-in mixer lift for easy accessibility when baking. For a unique kitchen island, I worked with our go-to craftsman for metalwork, Frank Wallace. We designed a rolled steel island narrow enough to fit the kitchen's new shape and still provide plenty of surface space for cooking. The black island gives such an unexpected contrast to all the neutral, earthy colors in the kitchen. Above the new stove, we wrapped the oven hood with material from the removed fireplace mantel, a rustic contribution to the look and feel of this space. A solid backsplash with an extended ledge, quartz countertops, and new flooring and lighting freshened up the newly opened kitchen. The stove hood, the steel island, and the custom cabinetry transformed this into a sleek and functional modern-lodge kitchen that now serves as the heart of this home.

JESSICA AND LEVI ARE professional restaurateurs and they requested a kitchen where they could cook and welcome in guests. They wanted to embrace their home's mid-century roots, but the original kitchen offered limited space and most of the original appliances barely worked. They also have two small children, so a room that connected easily to the rest of the house was paramount. They really needed a kitchen that fit their lifestyle. We removed cabi-

nets that blocked paths to the living areas and installed open shelving for easy access to plates and other often-used items. Subway tiles on the wall and wrapped around the range hood allowed for an easy-to-clean kitchen; an island/counter space provided room to eat as a family, or to host guests. We added a larger window over the sink so they could watch the kids play in the backyard. The end result was a sophisticated, mid-century modern kitchen fit for a family, and for a chef.

WE GAVE THIS KITCHEN a full overhaul by reorienting the space and replacing the cabinetry, flooring, and lighting. I chose a concrete trowel backsplash and concrete countertops to give the space a masculine, sophisticated twist in a house where the materials needed to be indestructible for Stan and his teenage sons. We added a special personal surprise: Dave built a hidden bourbon lift, set inside the island, which rises with the push of a button, ready to serve.

Dave's Corner

WOODEN TABLES AS WORKING ISLANDS

A lot of homes we work on are historic old houses, and space is at a premium. Practical, creative uses of space are a necessity whether you're in a small apartment or a larger house.

Recently, we've created a few kitchen islands from large wooden tables where the gas range is set right into the table, turning it into a useful, working part of the kitchen. The electric and gas lines run down through the table legs. It gives you that farmhouse table look, but it's modern and multifunctional. It's a cutting board, it's a cook top, it's an island.

CHAPTER 5

ORGANIZING

LAUNDRIES & PANTRIES

—

*Dancing in the
Laundry Room*

OUR FARMHOUSE WAS built in 1903. Back then, people had significantly less stuff than we do today. Closets were either nonexistent or very, very small. This constant battle for storage led us to remodel our home several years ago after we found out I was pregnant with our fifth child. Four years prior, we had downsized and moved into this old farmhouse as a family of four. We were now about to become a family of seven in a three-bedroom home and the simple truth was: We needed more space.

We had plans for a kitchen remodel and the addition of one extra bedroom. As we worked and reworked our designs, we decided to add a dormer to the upstairs playroom and convert the space into a fifth bedroom. Still, square footage was limited, and I stayed up late at night researching organization and storage tips from other big families. My preparation for this newest baby also included research on *how to keep up with the laundry created by a gaggle of children.* The ever-present and never-ending mounds of laundry in our closet-sized laundry room taunted me daily. The thought of adding a newborn's constant need for wardrobe changes to the laundry mix was the type of thing that made me panicky at 3:00 A.M. During my research, the term "family closet" kept appearing, and I was intrigued by the concept.

Essentially, a family closet is a room dedicated to closet and storage space for the entire family. Ideally, it's located near a laundry room and/or bathroom for convenience. I proposed the idea to Dave and suggested bumping out the side of our house to add on a room that could become a combined laundry room and family closet. We could build in "lockers" to serve as storage for each family member. Each of the lockers would have space for hanging clothes with drawers beneath.

It turns out, the family closet idea was a rather controversial topic (I won't mention names, but five out of six people in my family weren't on board with the concept). Admittedly, I had my own doubts about whether this would work. Still, we proceeded with my idea, knowing that built-in storage is always useful, and while

we might not end up using the room as a traditional family closet, we could certainly use the additional storage the new lockers would provide. In the course of the remodel, we were able to also add a small closet to each of the new bedrooms for the girls and to Luke's new nursery. The older boys share a room and a very small closet, so we included drawers in the new beds Dave built to serve as additional storage for them. This led me to wonder if we would actually use the family lockers and, if we did use them, what would we store in there versus in the closets in their rooms?

As I thought through how the lockers would serve each of us, I knew my personal locker would be most beneficial as an "out of season" storage space, particularly for the maternity clothes that were currently taking up temporary residence in my own small closet. I would move all my winter clothes into my locker, leaving space in my closet for maternity clothes and, eventually, only the clothing appropriate for a particular season that I wear every day. Dave would do the same for his space, and we both agreed to conduct a much-needed purge of our wardrobes be-

fore getting everything settled. I decided to use the opposite approach with the kids' lockers and closets. The plan was for their lockers to store everyday school clothes and sports uniforms, while their bedroom closets would store less-often-worn clothes like dressy attire, additional coats, and weekend play clothes.

When the remodel was finally complete and we moved back into our home, I was so excited about my new organizational system and couldn't wait to show it off to the kids. After the first week, they all refused to change their habit of getting ready in their own rooms and said they wanted to continue to use their bedroom closets instead of the new lockers in the laundry room.

My family closet seemed like a failure. However, after I started doing laundry in my pretty, newly remodeled laundry room, I decided to hang clean clothes in each kiddo's locker rather than walking each pile of clothes to individual rooms to be put away in the bedroom closets. The new system saved so much of my time—I simply hung as I unloaded the dryer, taking two steps to put clothes away in the appropriate locker instead of the typical routine of multiple trips to various bedrooms and back to the laundry room, on repeat. After I had hung the clothes in their lockers, I gave the kids the option to take out

all of their clothes, carry them upstairs, and put them away in their bedrooms, or leave the clothes in the locker and come downstairs in the morning to choose what to wear. Once they made their choice, they could change in the bathroom off the laundry room or in their individual bedrooms. They all chose to keep their clothes in the lockers, and we settled into a new routine.

Three years later, the system has evolved as the kids have gotten older. These days, either Dave or I wash and dry clothes and then we crank up the music and bring the kiddos in to retrieve anything that belongs to them. Sometimes there's complaining as we begin, but even the crankiest attitude doesn't stand a chance against an upbeat song and Dave's rendition of the Sprinkler with a pair of shorts on his head. Eventually we all end up singing and dancing together as everyone tackles the hanging, folding, and putting away of their own clothes. It takes a total of ten to fifteen minutes to finish the previously dreaded putting away of the laundry (we all know that throwing in a little detergent and pushing a button is the easy part . . . putting away the clothes is what's so awful).

Now, I would never rub it in or say the words *"I told you so"* but I will say, on a 1-to-10 scale of brilliant ideas, the combined family closet and laundry room is a 12. I have never been happier with any single addition to our home. The words "life changing" have been known to escape my lips. We have managed to save time and make the unavoidable chore of doing laundry a little less painful. Laundry happens every day in our house. And every day, we get a chance to model for our children that hard work can be beautifully intertwined with love in the form of dancing in the laundry room.

Intention

A PLACE FOR EVERYTHING

THE ORIGINAL LAUNDRY SPACE in this house had been in a closet across the hall. We chose to move it to an empty loft area to create a larger, open laundry room. We designed this house for a family, and when you have kids you are all inevitably in the laundry room together, whether you're pulling socks out of the dryer or somebody's searching for clothes before school. With the light-filled windows already in place, we added a sink to take advantage of the view, imagining that the house's future owners might have a small dog or two that could be washed in the sink. The decorative floor tiles added a playful element.

Jenny's Tip

LAUNDRY ROOM LAYOUT

Laundry room space is valuable and often overlooked when planning a home. While stacking the washer and dryer will help maximize space, planning for storage and folding areas is also helpful. Easily accessible storage for laundry supplies is useful, as is ample countertop space for folding and stacking clothes. A railing or retractable hanging/drying line is additionally useful, and a sink is one of the elements that works for some families, though not for others. If you wash a lot of clothes by hand or have small pets to bathe, it's useful, but a lot of times a sink can end up being a place where you throw clutter and piles of mail. You really have to evaluate whether you want a sink in your laundry room because it can take up a lot of counter space and you'll need to plan for the additional plumbing.

The danger with a laundry area is that it can easily become a magnet for clutter, castoffs, and piles of laundry. One way to counteract this is by making sure there is a home for everything. Another way is to make the space itself a place you really like to spend time in. A laundry room, like a powder bath, can be a place where you can have some design fun: paint the cabinets a bold color, install a cheerful wallpaper and beautiful floor tiles. This is a space we all spend a lot of time in so it's worth making it pretty. And, hopefully, the cheerful design will be a motivator to keep it (mostly!) in order.

NOT EVERYONE HAS the space for a separate pantry or a separate laundry, let alone both. We solved the need for both in this house by turning a former dining room off the kitchen into a walk-in pantry and new laundry room. We had chosen a warm blue for the kitchen cabinets, inspired by the owner's favorite element on the property: the old barn out back. In the barn, we found a gorgeous set of vintage doors the owner had been holding on to. Dave modified the doors to fit, and they created a charming entryway into the new pantry/laundry area.

TRISHA AND TODD WANTED an open kitchen, which required us to rework the floor plan and layout. After we removed a wall, we were able to create a spacious pantry and coffee station at the back of the newly reconfigured kitchen. I chose a dark, earthy shade of green for the kitchen cabinets and coffee station, and added warmth with an unfinished-wood open shelf. We installed a wooden counter-top in the pantry to save money and establish cohesiveness among all three spaces. The open pantry was hidden but easily accessible, with enough room for both useful and decorative items.

Dave

Hidden Spaces—Pantries

OVER THE YEARS, we've created a lot of hidden pantries. We've made some with two cabinet doors or two vintage doors that open to an expansive storage space with room to organize and store everything. A spacious hidden pantry can help get all your junk out of your kitchen, so you can see it all and access it more easily.

THIS HIDDEN WALK-IN PANTRY behind a beautiful vintage door provides ample storage. It was previously an unused space under the stairs. Dave and I love to repurpose hidden nooks into functional and unexpected spaces whenever possible.

WE ADDED THIS SMALL, tidy pantry as part of a kitchen redesign. It's no more than three by four feet, but the interior is large enough to easily store—and find—pantry staples. It has floor-to-ceiling shelving, which provides plenty of useful storage space. I love repurposing an antique door for a pantry entrance to add a focal point and warmth in a kitchen.

Jenny's Tip

USING OLD DOORS

Vintage doors are often not the size of a modern doorframe. When incorporating an old door into a home, it's important to know that the door may need to be modified. It is very possible to install an odd-sized door into a new home. You could use wider trim around a doorframe to accommodate a narrow door, or the base of the door can be cut to fit the new doorframe to accommodate a too-tall door. When possible, preserving the original hinges and hardware adds to the historic charm of an antique door.

CHAPTER 6

LIVING

FAMILY ROOMS &
OTHER SPACES FOR GATHERING

—

Christmas Morning

EVERY YEAR ON CHRISTMAS morning, Dave and I wake up before the sun rises and tiptoe out of our room and set to our tasks in silence, careful not to wake the still-sleeping kids upstairs. I quietly slip into the kitchen and turn on the coffee while Dave heads to the living room, where he stacks logs and lights a match to ignite a roaring fire. I join him in the living room, steaming mugs in hand, and we sit beneath a warm blanket in front of the fire. We sip coffee and listen to the sounds of the embers sparking and crackling. I look around and

soak in the picture-perfect scene: Gifts are wrapped and neatly piled under the tree with the soft glow of the Christmas lights and the amber cast of the fire illuminating the room in a dreamy haze.

Last year the tree itself was a tad lopsided and the branches sagged under the weight of the ornaments. It toppled over twice, soaking the rug and shattering a handful of ornaments. Even so, I can't bring myself to buy an artificial one. I love the fragrant natural pine scent of a live tree, and choosing the perfect tree as a family reminds me of my childhood. As a

kid, we had a very stringent "picking out the tree" tradition. On the Saturday after Thanksgiving, we would gather with my aunt Donna and her family at the Christmas tree section in the mall parking lot. The hunt for the perfect tree could take hours. We were very serious about what constituted the perfect tree and had to inspect each and every one on the lot. These days, my own kids carry on the tradition. They love to walk up and down each aisle of trees, fingertips grazing the blue-green Douglas fir needles. We sip hot cocoa and carefully analyze each tree. When we fi-

nally find the perfect one and load it onto the roof of the car to head home, I feel the same euphoric satisfaction that I've felt every year for as long as I can remember. We have the tree: The Christmas season can officially begin.

After the purchase of the tree, a flurry of frenzied activity begins. We haul the decor down from storage and reminisce together as we unwrap homemade and nostalgic ornaments. We decorate the tree and the house and make Christmas lists and bake cookies. We place baskets of homemade candies and cards on our neighbors' doorsteps. We visit Santa and drop letters to him at the North Pole mailbox in our little town square. We bundle up and join our friends at the Christmas parade. We shop for gifts and host parties. We read Advent devotionals and punch out little windows revealing tiny chocolates. We drive through town in search of the best Christmas lights display. We take photos and mail Christmas cards. We attend Christmas performances at school. We search for the mischievous little elf around the house each morning. We decorate the barn for Christmas Eve service. We wrap (and wrap and wrap) gifts. No matter how vigilant I am about keeping white space on our calendar in this season, it's inevitable that we go, go, go in the weeks leading up to Christmas.

Finally, after a peaceful and humble Christmas Eve service in our barn and a loud and jubilant dinner with family at Dave's parents' house, we make it home on Christmas Eve and pause together as a family. We pray and read the Christmas story aloud from the book of Luke. We let the kids unwrap a single gift from under the tree, set out cookies and milk, and then they settle into bed. Dave and I flutter around the house prepping for the morning and then finally collapse into a deep sleep well past midnight.

Even though we are lacking in sleep on Christmas morning, Dave and I are fueled by anticipation and joy. As we sit together in the whisper-quiet house, we exhale and rest in the stillness. This little Christmas morning ritual of ours is one I treasure. We turn on Christmas music, read scripture, and share our excitement over what gifts are under the tree and how we think the kids will react. We reminisce about past Christmases as the sun slowly rises and light streams in through the open curtains.

Soon after the sun's rays filter through

the windows, we hear tiny feet begin to scurry on the hardwood floor above us. The quiet morning is suddenly filled with excitement and activity. Little voices shout down from upstairs: *Can we come down?* I shout back to stay at the top of the stairs as I race to get my camera. Dave refills our coffee mugs, and we hear footsteps run from room to room, and voices yelling, *It's time! Wake up!* The kids know the drill: Everyone has to be awake and seated at the top of the stairs in order to come down together on Christmas morning. As soon as they're lined up, I snap the obligatory photo. The moment they hear the

click of the camera, they dash down the stairs. My shutter is clicking nonstop and the photos are inevitably blurry as they excitedly race past me toward the gifts under the tree.

Each year, we alternate who opens the first gift. Last year, it was Ben's turn. He took his time, looking through his small pile to decide which wrapped box would contain the best gift. He shook the boxes and held them in his hand, guessing what could be inside based on the weight. He finally selected a box that wasn't too small or too big. He probably thought it would be something electronic—a coveted gift for an eleven-year-old. Everyone watched as he ripped off the paper and tossed it aside, revealing a plain white box. Nathan cheered him on, knowing as his twin that whatever Ben was given would likely be in his pile as well. The collective gasps and sighs made me laugh out loud as Ben revealed the first present of the morning: two stacks of new (much needed, mind you) socks. He moaned dramatically and then joined in the chorus of laughter. The mornings go on like this, each kiddo taking a turn to open a gift while the rest of us look on and cheer as the new treasure is revealed. I encourage the kids to take their time. I take photos. Dave refills my coffee. We bask in the joy.

After all the gifts are unwrapped and everyone is contentedly playing with their new toys, Dave and I find our way back to the spot where we started: sipping coffee in front of the fire. Hours after we sat here at daybreak, I look around again and soak in the scene: The living room floor is now covered in discarded wrapping paper and ripped-open boxes are strewn about. The fire burns low and laughter and excited chatter fill the air. Eventually, we'll all pitch in to collect the trash, and toys and clothes will be put away. But, for now, I ignore the mess, turn up the festive music, and whisper a silent prayer of gratitude.

LETTING A SPACE BE DEFINED BY THE PEOPLE IN IT

FOR ANY HOME we work on, first and foremost we want it to be welcoming and warm. I found a beautiful muted pink, olive, and tan vintage rug to serve as the foundational first layer for this room. From there, I added a sofa and natural fiber chairs, along with a wooden sofa bench and a coffee table, which imparted texture and warmth.

Layout

TRANSFORMATIONAL TIP
Everything Starts with the Rug

If you are renovating or redesigning your living room, deciding on the rug is a great way to start to lay out the room. The rug sets off the space and creates the boundaries around which you can position your furniture. It should be big enough that it doesn't feel like a postage stamp, but not so big that it's hitting the edges of the room—just big enough so that all of the furniture can fit on or near its edges. The sofa can sit halfway on the rug, which is the same for chairs. The style of the rug sets the tone for the room, and rugs also offer a nice place to bring in color. I like to use vintage rugs— they're durable and the colors are often muted.

As a general rule, you don't want any of your seating to be more than eight to ten feet apart, otherwise people will need to talk loudly to hear one another. If you have a big space to fill, you might want to create smaller seating areas off the main area where people can sit closer, and side or nesting tables can be used as resting surfaces.

WHEN WE TRANSFORMED A hundred-year-old barn into a home, we wanted to reincorporate as much of the original exterior wood as possible. The wood has been oxidizing for a century and has the perfect amount of warmth for walls and beams. This new living room feels rustic, warm, and inviting with the barn wood on the walls and the stone fireplace as the central focal point. The formal chandelier is on a dimmer and adds a sophisticated elegance that balances the natural elements in this space.

Jenny's Tip

THE COFFEE TABLE

The coffee table is often the undersung hero of a living room. It's an important, central piece of furniture that's not always considered in the overall furniture plan. Dave will often make coffee tables for me because I'm very particular about the size, type of material, and height.

I don't have a hard-and-fast rule for the shape of a coffee table, but I do like the scale to be proportionate to the sofa. With a sectional and chaise, a rectangular coffee table works best, while a full sectional or even an L-shaped couch works well with round nesting tables. With two sofas, a rectangular table is typically best again. In all cases, the table ideally shouldn't be longer than two-thirds of the length of the sofa. I prefer natural wood coffee tables, although I will use an iron coffee table or a metal-and-glass table for a modern living room. I don't often use glass tables in homes with small children, as they're harder to keep clean and not kid friendly.

A spacious walking area around the table helps the space flow nicely, though the table

needs to be close enough to the sofa or chairs to be easily reachable by anyone sitting on the furniture. If a coffee table is too tall, too low, or too far away from the sofa, the entire furniture configuration feels off. The table needs to be the right height, which is slightly lower than the seating. Typically, a table should be around sixteen to eighteen inches tall for a standard sofa with a seat height of twenty inches.

Jenny's Tip

LIGHTING AREAS & LIGHTING SOURCES

For a living room, I prefer either a chandelier or a ceiling fan to help define the space. Ceiling fans aren't the most aesthetically pleasing but they are functional, and most families prefer one in a room they relax in and use often. Overhead lights on dimmers are wonderful for easily adjusting the mood in the room—from bright, direct light needed for reading to softer, more atmospheric lighting. Of course, natural light is always my first preference.

Table lamps are invaluable in a living room because they bring in warmth and versatility. The light they cast is often flattering and sets a soft mood in the space. I like to hide the cords as much as possible behind side tables or sofas near a wall. If the sofa is in the center of the room, I run the cord under the rug to conceal it as best I can.

Focal Points

Every living room needs a focal point. Whether it is a built-in bookshelf, a great piece of art, a fireplace, or a beautiful view, a focal point helps to organize the furniture in the space.

Fireplaces

HERE WE ADDED large-scale windows to flank the fireplace and flood the space with natural light. Dave created a fireplace with rolled steel panels as the focal point; he even stayed late one night to grind and buff the steel with car wax to make it shine. The panels will naturally oxidize over time, changing color and helping to create a gorgeous, airy modern living room.

THIS LAKESIDE CABIN (right) was cramped and dark before we vaulted the ceiling to accentuate the original pitch of the roof. Now the space feels much larger, and the new wood paneling adds warmth and texture. To complete the cozy cabin-in-the-woods feel, we added stone to the previously run-of-the-mill brick fireplace and installed an organic mantel made from driftwood found along the lakeshore. This is the perfect spot for cozying up under a wool blanket in front of a roaring fire.

Artwork

THIS HOME WAS ORIGINALLY built by the homeowner's grandparents and has been in the family for generations. Over the years, the family portraits had been collected and stored away. We brought these beautiful paintings out to display on the new mantle in a modern take on the traditional gallery wall.

A LOCAL ARTIST NAMED Buddy Whitlock painted this custom mural, incorporating Bentonville landmarks into a beautiful piece of art.

TO HONOR THE homeowner's Peruvian heritage, we created a wall of texture using hand-woven baskets as the focal point within the new built-ins in the living room. This is an example of how untraditional art can be created using well-loved or nostalgic items.

Jenny's Tip

THE THREE S'S—
STORAGE, SHELVING
& SURFACE AREAS

STORAGE: You can never have enough storage in any home. Anywhere that you can add hidden or out-of-the-way storage in a living area is helpful, whether it is a place to conceal crafting items, the TV remotes, books, or children's toys.

SHELVING: Open shelving can display cherished items. Built-in cabinets can be storage for treasured books. These serve as both storage and a way to add decorative detail and visual interest.

SURFACE AREAS: Different heights of open surface areas, such as end tables, sideboards, and firm ottomans, can add versatility to a space. Pocket, nested, and other moveable small tables increase surface area possibilities, whether that means a small table where guests can place their drinks or an open surface where lovely trinkets or family photos can be displayed.

Jenny's Tip

PERSONAL TOUCHES

When you have open shelving and surface areas in a living room, you should display things that are meaningful, while maintaining white space, varied heights, and well-thought-out spacing so each piece can be enjoyed visually both by itself and in relation to the objects around it. You don't want everything to be the same height and shape, so you need to mix and match and play around, then step back and live with it for a minute. It's not an exact science, but the key is to make sure surfaces and open shelving are not overly stuffed. The things you are displaying should be things that you love and that have meaning. In our house, we have a collection of rocks and shells from places we've traveled to. We label the rocks with the place and date, and keep them in a bowl on the shelf—a constant reminder of our wonderful adventures together.

Jenny's Tip

WALL MOLDING

I like to use wall molding where it makes sense. It can add visual interest and a nice architectural detail, but if you're in a modern home or a Craftsman home, it just doesn't mesh. If you have an old Victorian house, adding molding with raised panel walling can create beautiful feature walls that are in keeping with the integrity of the house.

The Welcome Inn is an old Victorian home and so it felt appropriate to install molding in the spacious living room. With so much light coming in through the large windows, the molding both suited the style of the house and imparted an elevated feel to the room.

CHAPTER 7

ENTERTAINING

OUTDOOR SPACES, PATIOS, SCREENED-IN PORCHES & OTHER INDOOR GATHERING PLACES

Movie Night

IN APRIL 2016, I RECEIVED AN email from a programming executive at HGTV who was wondering if we would be interested in discussing a show idea. Assuming the email was spam, I deleted it and moved on until a friend who had passed along our information to the network confirmed that it was, in fact, a real person emailing me. Dave encouraged me to dig it out of the trash folder and tentatively respond, both of us very much unsure if this was a path we wanted to pursue. Over a cup of coffee with a development producer who grew up in our town, we were eventually convinced. The producer assured us that he would never want to portray this place we love in anything but the best possible light.

Over the course of the next three and a half years, Dave and I worked to develop and film eleven episodes of what would become the pilot and then the first season of *Fixer to Fabulous*. Although the work was intense and the days were long, we felt extremely grateful for this wild, unexpected, and uncharted adventure. Postproduction took longer than expected, delaying the series premiere by a full year.

After waiting months for news, we finally got the call letting us know that the series was set to premiere on October 22, 2019.

The owner of our local movie theater offered the space for us to watch our first episode on the big screen together with friends. Dave and I invited everyone who had helped us along the way. That night, we gathered in the theater with our family, friends, homeowners, and the production crew, who had become like family to us. We ate fancy food, toasted bubbly champagne, and shared stories of the journey leading to that unforgettable evening. Then, we all sat together, snacking on popcorn and laughing as we watched two

months of our life edited down into forty-two minutes of television. It was a surreal, magical blur of a night—a big, beautiful celebration of the culmination of years of hard work. My cheeks hurt from smiling by the end of it. That little movie theater will forever be tied to dazzling, joyful memories.

Less than five months after that evening, the world shut down because of the pandemic. The mounting fear and uncertainty around the virus permeated everyone's lives. The world had changed in an instant and we were all living in a very strange, new existence together. For a brief period, humanity—with all of our differ-

ences and cultural realities—felt surprisingly united. Our quarantine routines and daily lives varied—some of us were strictly homebound, some were working as essential employees—yet the thing that united us all was the fact that our cities and towns and "normal" daily lives suddenly looked drastically different.

As a mom of five very little, very impressionable hearts and minds, I was single-minded in my attempt to protect my kids from the headlines. Dave and I were truthful with them about what was happening in the world, but in an age-appropriate way. We talked openly about our anxious thoughts and concerns. We prayed often. We checked in constantly. I was hell-bent against allowing fear to grip their hearts. Seemingly overnight, our jam-packed calendar cleared. So many good things—like field trips and sports games and art camps—were canceled. The normal busy spring schedule we maintained slowed dramatically. While we collectively mourned the loss of many good things, our family of seven made a very intentional effort to embrace and appreciate the slower pace of each day. We had no need to rush into bedtime routines in anticipation of early mornings, allowing us to take long walks and play games and watch movies together. We read books on

the porch swing and cheered as baby Luke tried to stand on his wobbly little legs.

A persistent lament in our family was how desperately we missed our people. By nature, our family is all about hospitality and opening our home to loved ones. During a typical spring season, our house is a revolving door of friends and family coming by for dinner or stopping over for coffee on the front porch. We *love* our people, and we adore sitting around the table for hours of laughter and conversations and good food. As the months of quarantine dragged on, we were forced to get creative and find new ways to connect with our community.

On the Saturday before Easter, we ran around town hiding eggs in the kids' friends' yards and left baskets of candy and champagne on the porch for their parents before honking the horn and slowly driving away. The kids leaned out the car windows as they waved and shouted, "Happy Easter!" as soon as a surprised friend opened their front door. For Charlotte and the twins' birthdays that summer, we held "birthday parades" instead of traditional parties. We decorated the end of our driveway with balloons and a giant sign in the yard and sent invitations to friends and family. On their birthdays, Charlotte and then the boys stood outside beaming and waving as their friends slowly drove

past our house, honking horns and tossing gifts and the occasional water balloon our way.

Because the movie theater was closed, we couldn't keep our annual end-of-summer tradition of a movie night with friends. So we got creative. A friend had purchased a large outdoor movie screen, so I asked her if we could set it up in our yard. She surprised us with a setup of string lights and lanterns and comfy chairs for the kids. After a blissful day of swimming under the scorching August sun, we invited one of our "quarantine families" to join us for an outdoor movie night. Despite the fact that we weren't eating popcorn and watching the big screen in a theater like we had done so many times before, we didn't miss that tradition in the least. This new one, a movie night under the stars, was pure magic. The uncertainty of the world felt far away, and the innocence of childhood was alive and well under twinkly lights in our yard that night.

Sometimes, nurturing friendships is simple and easy. However, in some seasons, life is complicated and hard. And it's in those seasons when we need our people the most. Something I've always told my kids (which has felt more relevant than ever these past couple of years) is that I don't ever expect perfect grades or blue ribbons or first-place trophies. While I want my children to understand the value of hard work, I never want them to get so caught up in achievements and accolades that they lose sight of what's really important in this life: relationships. Without the people we love and the memories we create *together,* our life lacks purpose and joy and significance. When we take the time to set up a screen in the yard and invite a couple of friends over for a silly movie about a cartoon dog, we teach our kids the importance of prioritizing relationships and fighting for community.

Intention

ENCOURAGING JOYFUL TIMES
& HAPPY MEMORIES

WE ARE SO FORTUNATE to have fairly mild seasons here in Northwest Arkansas, which allowed me to design this space for the Gheen family to enjoy year-round (with a few blankets and an extra log on the fireplace in the winter). I chose antique brick salvaged from a local building for the fireplace and Dave built a mantel out of milled catalpa wood (which is very resistant to decay) from an old tree out front. We flanked the fireplace with crepe myrtles that the owner loved and added horizontal wood post fencing to create warmth and give the owners some privacy. The space is now so inviting and cozy, I don't think I would ever leave my spot right in front of that burning fireplace!

TRANSFORMATIONAL TIP

Planning an Outdoor Entertaining Space

When you begin planning an outdoor entertaining space, consider the sun, the climate, the weather, and the seasons. What time of day will you most often want to use it? Will you need shade? If you want to use the space in the evenings, will a fireplace or a firepit give you enough warmth? Do you want to be able to cook and eat outdoors? Outdoor kitchen or grilling area? Tree cover or umbrella? Lounging furniture or dining tables? The options are many, and it's not about either/or, but instead about determining what works for your lifestyle and how you see yourself using the space. How you want to use the space is as important as taking into account the weather, the climate, and the seasons.

Outdoors

WE UPDATED THIS old boat dock to make it a multi-functional and beautiful spot. First, we rethought the kayak and fishing storage areas, then extended the roofline to create a covered outdoor bar. I personally love the antique canoe Dave turned into a light fixture. He suspended it with shipping rope above the trough bar sink that keeps drinks ice cold while guests are fishing off the dock. Dave even built a spot for an outdoor TV. The owner had dreamed of a firepit with Adirondack chairs, so I enlisted our neighbor (who specializes in custom metal work) to create one with a custom cutout inspired by a nautical heirloom the home-owner cherishes. The space is now perfect for multi-seasonal lakeside entertaining.

FOR THIS CABIN, we wanted the entertaining area to be modern, yet timeless. We built a brand-new deck with multiple seating areas where everyone could gather cozily around the new fireplace and enjoy the views of the nearby lake. We added these personalized vintage oars that my little artist, Nathan, helped me create.

PAUL, THE OWNER OF this house, had already made a lot of progress with the backyard when he brought us in. We needed only to add a few more features to make it even better for entertaining. A fun focal point for the outdoor seating area is the large outdoor fireplace where guests can convene and warm up on cooler nights.

THIS FAMILY LOVES to have people over and spends a lot of time outside. To create a functional entertaining space, we built a deck with an outdoor kitchen for grilling that we situated for maximum enjoyment of the property's extraordinary lake view. Using white oak, Dave built Adirondack chairs—one for each of the family members, including two child-sized chairs (what is it about a child-sized chair that makes me swoon? I love them so much!). Now each member of the family has a seat where they can enjoy the lake.

Jenny's Tip

INSPIRING WITH WORDS

Sometimes we all need a bit of inspiration to get us through the day and remind ourselves of a bigger perspective. While I don't do it often, and don't do it only in outside spaces—we once added "Lookin' Good" to the floor of a cute little bathroom—here are a few places we added some inspiration to outdoor spaces we've designed.

This is a phrase that homeowner Madison heard a lot from her dad growing up. And why not? It's a great philosophy for life.

The owner of this house had recently recovered from a difficult illness and dreamed of a quiet reading place. We created a brand for her porch swing—"Laura's Chair"—which included the Bible verse Isaiah 26:4: "Trust in the Lord forever, for the Lord, the Lord himself, is the Rock eternal." (NIV)

When Dave's mom went through breast cancer, I gave her a necklace with "Isaiah 26:4" engraved on it. The verse was a comfort for her, and I hope it has been one for Laura.

Indoors/Outdoors

WHEN WE FIRST BOUGHT the property that we've turned into the Welcome Inn, we went back and forth on how to use the old concrete outbuilding. From the very beginning we called it "The Smokehouse" because Dave thought it could be really cool to smoke meat in there if we used the house as a bed-and-breakfast. Our guests could have fresh bacon. Eventually, as the inn evolved, we thought the space would be better utilized as an outdoor kitchen before finally settling on the idea that our guests could best use it as an indoor/outdoor dining area.

July 1958

I LOVE THE ORIGI-NAL concrete of the building, so we kept it and the original ceiling. We cut out some windows to provide natural light and added basket pendants and fun string lighting to turn on when it gets dark outside. The racquets on the wall were a last-minute idea when I was out shopping for the house. I saw some vintage racquets and thought they could make a fun, playful art piece. We want to encourage people to have fun out there, and the racquets add a little bit of whimsy.

This is the first space in which we tried out a prototype of the table design Dave built for our outdoor furniture line. It fit the space perfectly even though we'd not planned it that way. The Smokehouse turned into a bit of an experimental lab as we designed our outdoor line. The seating in front of the building also includes some of our lanterns and planters.

THIS WAS A UNIQUE renovation to find in our area, one with a pool house on the property. We painted the exterior the same shade of black as the main house and installed a new garage door that could be opened to give the pool house an outdoor feel in nice weather. We also resurfaced the inside of the pool, installed new tile, and added a little bar area. As a fun, funky element and a nod to the 1970s—the era when it was built—a friend painted a graphic mural on the wall. I've never been able to incorporate a disco ball into a renovation before, and for that reason alone, this may be one of my favorite spaces to date!

JENNY'S FAVORITE PAINT COLORS

JENNY'S FAVORITE PAINT COLORS

Entertaining Space

Farrow & Ball Plummet

Sherwin-Williams Pewter Green

Farrow & Ball Setting Plaster

Farrow & Ball Pigeon

Benjamin Moore Kendall Charcoal

Farrow & Ball Drop Cloth

Indoors

THIS SPACE WAS ORIGINALLY a laundry room off a kitchen that the owner, Paul, didn't really use. We relocated the washer and dryer and made the space into a hidden speakeasy. I think this might be one of Dave's favorite projects. Since the owner loves bourbon, Dave built a steel shelving unit with several cubbies to display his bourbon collection. I painted the entire space, including the ceiling, a dark charcoal with blue undertones. This is a great example of how a dark, bold color can make a small space feel dramatic, yet warm and cozy.

DAVE CREATED a floor-to-ceiling wine rack just off of the entryway and living room in my sister's house, which is both visually striking and convenient for entertaining.

WE CREATED THIS ROOM off the first-floor dining room in the Welcome Inn and have been calling it the Bourbon Room. We wanted it to be a place to have a predinner drink or listen to music after a meal. I painted the floors and ceilings to make it feel dark and cozy and lit it with atmospheric wall sconces. The leather club chairs add a sophisticated lounge vibe. We added built-ins to store games and puzzles, and I repurposed some beautiful old card catalog file boxes that I found at an antiques store into bourbon storage.

Dave

"We Built the Biggest Table We Could"

THE CELLAR AREA of the Welcome Inn was a large, awkward space that we wanted to find a good use for. Jenny likes to create spaces where you can have big gatherings so people can come together for causes, or just as families. We thought guests could use it for cozy dinners, and when the inn is empty, we could also use it for fundraising events.

The room is a rectangle: long, but not super wide. A tornado tore through our property and knocked down trees on our farm. I had the trees milled and have used the wood for several projects; I knew the remaining oak beams would work perfectly for this table. I wanted a steel base because the table is in an old cellar that gets wet and I didn't want wood touching the floor. My dad and brother helped me build the biggest table we could. We made a twelve-foot-long table that's four feet wide and fills almost the whole room so that lots of people can gather around it. Building the table with my dad and brother made it that much more meaningful to me.

WE CREATED THIS SPACE in the basement of the Welcome Inn out of an old storage room. The exposed brick walls and flooring give the room great texture and atmosphere. Dave built wine racks, cabinets, and a buffet table for serving. I chose the soft rose velvet chairs because the color and elevated materials are unexpected and balance the moody space. With all the wood and the brick floor, they add a little plush, elegant comfort to the harder surfaces and textures of the room.

CHAPTER 8

THE NECESSITIES

BATHROOMS—SHOWERS, BATHTUBS, VANITIES & POWDER BATHS

—

the Hundred-Year-Old Tub

OUR FARMHOUSE WAS originally located in our town's historic area, near our picturesque downtown square. When Dave learned it was set to be demolished, he came up with a plan to save it. He hired a house-moving company—a type of business I never knew existed before this—and we prepared to physically pick up the house and move it across town to a little plot of land. Eventually the house would be settled on a hill overlooking a pond, with pastures and farms as far as the eye can see.

The actual process of moving the house was extensive. It took several months to secure the permits and prepare the house. The main floor was placed on steel I beams and hauled away by a semitruck. The second floor had been removed and cut into three sections before being driven to the property. The move itself occurred very early on a Sunday morning to ensure the roads would be clear of traffic. It took almost three hours to get the house across town. The boys, only two years old at the time, drowsy from sleep and wearing their warm footie pajamas, cheered from the car as the three of us watched the house drive along, Dave standing in the road, directing the trucks. When it came time to turn down our little dirt road, Dave and the house movers realized it was too narrow. Dave spoke to our new neighbor, Bob, who was watching the unusual Sunday commotion. Bob agreed to remove a fence to allow the trucks to drive the house across his pasture. The boys cheered again as the house slowly moved across the grass. Suddenly the procession stopped as the weight of the trucks began to sink into the soil. Dave hopped into his bulldozer to pull the trucks one by one over to the foundation that had been poured earlier. The second level was placed back onto the house and reconstructed. After the foundation of the house and the walls and roof were secure, we began the long process of remodeling it.

We took our time with the restoration, slowly getting to know the house. We spent hours and hours walking the rooms, running our hands along the walls, peeling back linoleum tiles, drawing up plans, and dreaming about how we would reconfigure walls or where we could find the extra thirty square feet needed to replace the existing spiral staircase with a regular staircase. One thing we knew for certain was that we wanted to keep as much of the house's integrity and as many of its original features as we could. We loved the quirky angles and the charming old doors with wobbly doorknobs. We were delighted to uncover original ceiling joists in the kitchen that had been hidden under layers of acoustic tiles and Sheetrock over the years, and agreed the joists needed to remain exposed.

In the first-floor bathroom, we unanimously voted to keep the cast-iron clawfoot bathtub. The tub was originally cast in 1903 and, while it's smaller than a modern tub, it belongs here, and I absolutely adore it. The tub remains in the same bathroom where it has sat for more than a hundred years. And in this tub, right after we moved in, the boys each took their first bath in the new house, resulting in a wet floor from water splashing over the rim. In this tub, two months after we moved in, I gently nestled a baby sling for Charlotte's first newborn bath. In this tub, shivering kids soak in steamy water to defrost after playing in the snow each winter. In this tub, in desperation, I handed over water paint and brushes and let three-year-old Charlotte create a masterpiece in the middle of a blustery cold day. In this tub, miniature tugboats and rubber ducks and plastic dinosaurs have gone on countless epic adventures at sea.

In this tub is where, on the night Sylvie came home, at two and a half years old, she took her first warm bath. In the Congo, where running water is scarce and the tub was never filled, she was used to standing for infrequent showers while cold water was poured over her with a small cup. On that first night under our roof, I turned on the faucet and encouraged her to sit down. She refused. Instead, she stood in our hundred-year-old tub and curiously reached out her little hand to touch the water flowing from the tap. As the warm water grazed her fingertips, she jumped back, startled. Slowly, she reached her hand out again to feel the stream. As she let the unusually warm water run over her hand, a broad smile of delight spread across her face. From that moment on, she absolutely loved bath time. As the months went on, she learned to sit and relax in that tub. Whenever she was having a hard day or feeling afraid or anxious, I would turn on the water. Instantly, the sound of the rushing water would soothe her. She would soak and play in the tub for hours during that first year at home. The sounds of water splashing and her deep belly laughter created a beautiful, melodic harmony.

When I was a kid, my mom would draw a warm bath with lavender-scented bubbles whenever I wasn't feeling well. It was comforting, and, to this day, a whiff of lavender reminds me of that sense of warmth and safety. My meemaw taught my nana who taught my mom who taught me to believe in the power of a good detox bath. It remains my first line of defense whenever an illness strikes our home. My

kids all know that if they start to feel like a sickness is coming on, I'll immediately draw them a bath. I'll fill the tub with hot water and a cupful of Epsom salt, half a cupful of baking soda, a dash of apple cider vinegar, a tablespoon of ginger, and a few drops of lavender oil. There's a healing power within the water and the salts and the oils.

To this day, the bath is the place I go to soak and let the worries of the day dissipate as sore muscles loosen and relax. When I have had a particularly long day or when I feel run-down, Dave will take over whatever I'm working on and gently insist that I take a bath. He knows that a soak in hot water with dim candlelight and a good book can reset my attitude and physically restore me. Often, evenings are chaotic with five kids and a farm full of animals to attend to, yet, when I take the time for a seemingly self-indulgent soak in the tub, I find myself calmer and more at peace and better able to sleep at night.

Yes, the bath is primarily a place for good hygiene and cleaning off the dirt and grime from a long day. But, most important, this old tub of ours has been a place for healing and a soothing source of calm for our family. I like to think it has done the same for the many decades of families that came before us.

MAKING BEAUTIFUL SPACES OUT OF NECESSARY PLACES

WE REORIENTED THIS lake house bathroom to create a large vanity and shower area. I chose accessories that would look handmade and natural against the backdrop of the outdoors and the lake.

TRANSFORMATIONAL TIP
Arches & Alcoves

Using or creating arches and alcove areas can introduce architectural features that add a sense of grandeur and character, like what you might see in an old home in Europe. You can find similar spaces in many older houses in America—a hundred-year-old house will often have alcoves and odd angles,

which I love. Arches and alcoves add visual interest and create inviting spaces, and they can breathe fresh life into what would otherwise be an ordinary bathroom.

Shower Areas

TRANSFORMATIONAL TIP *Tile Choices*

Tile sizes and shapes can set the tone for an entire bathroom. There are endless options—octagon, square, penny, subway shapes and colors, finishes, and textures—each one helping to create a different style.

IF YOU WANT A classic look, rectangular subway-style tile is a traditional choice that always works well. In this case I used a subway tile with a modern twist by installing it in a "soldier stack" pattern. The vertical install and bold hand-glazed blue tile create a varied, mosaic feel.

FOR THIS SHOWER, I chose gorgeous hand-thrown tiles and had them installed in a stacked vertical pattern. I love to use handmade tiles because they are made from natural materials and are inconsistent in size and shape. I love that no two tiles are the same. Their beautiful imperfections create instant character and texture.

LIGHTER-COLORED TILING can be more timeless, but if you love color, shower tile is a great place to incorporate it. The owner of this bathroom loves pink, and we found just the right shade for a unique contrasting tone to the concrete floor. The use of a slightly elongated rectangular subway tiling fit well with this home's sophisticated aesthetic. The clear shower door ensured that the pink tile remained the focal point in the completely remodeled bathroom.

IN THIS SHOWER AREA, the juxtaposition of colors, finishes, sizes, and shapes of the three different tile choices created lovely visual variety and added textural appeal that helped to transform it from feeling purely utilitarian to a Mediterranean spa–inspired space.

I BELIEVE A smaller bathroom is the perfect place to have a little fun with design. In this bathroom, I created a unique and colorful mosaic tile pattern as the focal point of the space. I wanted the tile to be an unexpected contrast to the traditional wall molding. The handcrafted sconces, sink, and faucet add a timeless element to the bathroom. Dave built a gorgeous black walnut cabinet for storage that completes the classic and character-filled space.

TRANSFORMATIONAL TIP
Plumbing Fixture Choices

Like tiling, the choice of plumbing fixtures in bath, shower, and vanity areas can make strong statements and shape how the overall space feels. Both chrome and black plumbing fixtures are modern choices, while brushed gold gives a warmth and a lovely softness. Natural unlacquered brass is always my preference for plumbing and hardware. However, brass is going to age: The color will change the more it is touched and used. While you can polish it, you must be willing to embrace the change in color if the finish is not sealed.

IN THIS SPACE, I used black fixtures that work well with the light tile. The deep bathtub makes it a perfect place to relax and unwind.

IN THIS BATHROOM I used fixtures with a brass finish, adding an eye-catching touch that helps pull the space together.

Jenny's Tip

SMALL CHANGES THAT MAKE A BIG IMPACT

While changing tiling and lighting placement is not easy, changing lighting fixtures and cabinet hardware is, and can be a quick way to transform the feel of a bathroom. If you are not planning a full bathroom renovation, swapping out what can be easily changed can really impact the overall look of the space. For instance, replacing a rectangular vanity mirror with an arched or oval one, or vice versa, will have a larger impact than you might expect. Using thinner woven rugs in place of bath mats can bring in color and elevate the look of a bathroom space. Updating cabinet hardware is a simple way to refresh the look of a bathroom vanity and can make a big statement.

Vanities

Jenny's Tip

ONE OR TWO SINKS? DOORS OR DRAWERS?

When you are planning your vanity area, make sure to spend time thinking about how your household will use it. How much counter space do you need versus how much sink space? These days, the tendency can be to assume two sinks are always

the best option, but unless two people will often be using the area at the same time, a single sink may work just as well and also give you extra counter space.

Also consider what kind of storage you need and how you want to access it. Do you prefer your things stored in drawers or behind doors? It is mainly personal preference, though I do think drawers make things more easily visible, while cupboards are good for bulkier cleaning supplies, bathroom supplies, and extra towels.

WE CREATED THIS gorgeous spa-like bathroom as part of a main bedroom suite for my sister. We installed floating oak cabinets that echo cabinetry used elsewhere in the house. The wooden vertical slat tile added a modern, warm, and unexpected touch to the bathroom. This is probably my favorite floor tile of all time, and I love how it runs all the way up the wall to create visual interest.

THE DOUBLE SINKS in this floating vanity offer a modern feel when paired with the bold green tile that I also used in the shower area of this bathroom.

THIS HOME WAS built in the early 1900s and the homeowners wanted to keep as much original character as possible while incorporating their affinity for modern design. In the main bathroom, I leaned into the modern aesthetic with sophisticated wall sconces but dark hardware and kept the vanity a natural wood finish to infuse a timeless warmth.

Dave's Corner

TRANSFORMING OLD FURNITURE INTO VANITIES

Making old dressers into vanities works really well for the right space. All dressers are pretty much the same depth. The width is the thing you've got to look for. Once we know the width of the space we have, Jenny goes out and finds the piece of furniture.

You can use a vessel sink, like Jenny often does, or you can cut out the space for a drop-in sink. Typically, an old dresser has three to four drawers. In the first two drawers you'll need to cut the backs off and nail them shut so they're no longer functional. In the bottom drawer you may have to notch out the actual drawer itself so that it can fit the plumbing pipes that have to drop through the sink, but it'll still hold soap and toilet paper and other bathroom necessities.

Powder Baths

Jenny's Tip

WALLPAPER FOR
POWDER BATHS

I love powder baths. They are a perfect place to have some design fun. One of my favorite elements to use is bold and beautiful wallpaper. The smaller size of a powder bath is a wonderful opportunity to focus on charming details: carefully chosen or personally designed wallpaper that adds lots of visual interest, simple wooden trims that complement the intricacy of many wallpapers, and the more intimate dimensions of smaller sink basins.

I WAS INSPIRED BY a ginkgo tree on the Welcome Inn property to create a custom wallpaper for the first-floor bathroom. I worked with Kelly Ventura, an incredibly talented artist, who created this beautiful wallpaper based on the tree's unique leaf structure.

THE LIGHTING AND MIRROR are really toned down in this powder bath because I wanted the sink and faucets to be the main focal points. The sink is handmade, wall-mounted, and cast in concrete. The faucets are brass and hand forged. The Saltillo floor tile is also handmade and complements the Spanish feel of the sink. The small room doesn't have any windows.

People are often afraid to use a dark paint in a small room because they think it will make it feel even smaller, but I think the dark color increases the coziness and makes a bold statement. The deep green color helps to make this small bathroom pretty and sophisticated.

CHAPTER 9

WORKING, MAKING & DOING

HOME OFFICES & STUDIES, SHOPS & STUDIOS

—

the Sofa & the Shop

SHORTLY AFTER WE MOVED to the farm, we built a garage with a small apartment above it to serve as a space for visitors. The bedroom stays ready for overnight guests, while the living room has become a catchall storage spot for our extra stuff. I keep a bin of wrapping paper in the closet alongside the kids' artwork that I need to frame. There's a basket filled with extra blankets and pillows next to an exercise bike that I've used twice. Under the bed, I stash extra vases and bowls and platters stacked and ready for a dinner party. I also have a really comfy sofa up there because I had a spontaneous idea last summer to turn the apartment into a movie room. I found a sectional with deep seats and fluffy cushions that beckons you to curl up with a warm blanket. I never got around to buying a projector to complete the movie room, but I'm really glad I added the sofa because it has become my favorite writing spot.

In our old house, I had a chair in the corner of the living room where I would

begin each day. I would sit with my Bible, journal, and a steaming mug of coffee for a few minutes or a few hours, depending on my schedule. I could think clearly in that chair. When we moved to the farmhouse, the chair didn't fit, and I couldn't quite find that magical little spot inside. The front porch is where I start most mornings now, and it has become my favorite place to do so. But since we've added the sofa to the apartment, you'll often find me there typing away on my laptop or scribbling down thoughts in my journal. It's quiet up there, I can look out

the windows, and, as long as I ignore the random boxes full of photos I need to sort through and extra rugs stowed in the corner, I can think most clearly from this cozy little perch.

While I'm usually found upstairs, hiding away, tucked under a blanket, scrambling to write down my thoughts before the rest of the house awakens, you will most often find Dave in his woodshop out in the barn, covered in sawdust, classic rock streaming through the speakers of his twenty-year-old boom box, creating something. He spends hours in the place he has specifically carved out to channel his creativity. The kids often join him, and each has their own little section in the shop. Luke knows he can find his miniature hammer, goggles, and screwdriver in the far drawer on the right; the girls keep their pink toolboxes on the first shelf; and Ben and Nate are now old enough to work alongside Dave whenever they meander out to the shop to see what he's working on.

Dave has quite literally built every piece of wooden furniture in our home out in his shop. He built all our beds, including Luke's crib, the tables and end tables and coffee table, the TV cabinet and nightstands. He welded the handrail on our staircase and built all of the picture frames and shelves and cutting boards. I'm constantly astounded at how he can spend a couple of hours in his shop and emerge with a gorgeous piece of furniture.

One Easter morning a couple of months before Luke was due to be born, the kids gave me the most adorable wooden toys for their new baby brother. There were two cars from the boys and an elephant and a stack of wooden rings from the girls. The week before, they had each spent an afternoon learning to draw, cut, rout, and sand their toy in the shop with Dave patiently guiding the work. When they proudly handed me their wrapped toys on Easter morning, I teared up with gratitude. The time and love they'd poured into these gifts for their new brother was not lost on me. The toys were proudly displayed in Luke's nursery, joyfully anticipating his arrival.

These days, the cars have a few nicks and the elephant's tail is slightly frayed from use. The visible signs of how well loved they are makes them even more special. I imagine Luke's own babies playing with these same toys someday. They'll become heirlooms that represent what is valued most in our family—hard work, creativity, and generosity. They're made to spark imaginative play and were lovingly shaped by little hands willing to make something special for someone they hadn't even met yet. To me, that is the heart of generosity: expending your time and talents and resources for someone else.

Dave and I are big proponents of being creative with your home and making the most of the spaces within. Traditional offices with bookshelves and a desk are wonderful, but a cozy sofa and a sawdust-lined workshop are just as effective for the two of us. We love our unique spots where we can make things and contribute in our own small ways to the world. The words I write and the pieces Dave builds are tangible gifts for our family. I write down our family's stories like touchstones, as a way to remember all that God has done for us. And Dave builds pieces like our kitchen table, where we can gather together to create new stories just waiting to be recorded.

Intention

ENABLING PRODUCTIVITY & ENCOURAGING CREATIVITY

Work

WE CONVERTED AN unused front bedroom into this light-flooded, eye-catching study for its owners, Cynthia and Scotty Cooper. The striking color of the back wall contrasts beautifully with lighter details in the rest of the room. I firmly believe that homes should reflect the people who live in them: Cherished, meaningful family heirlooms need to be incorporated into the design. I dug this beautiful antique desk out of Cynthia's storage and refurbished it for her new study. It was an emotional moment for Cynthia when she saw that we'd transformed this treasured heirloom into something that she could use and enjoy every day.

Jenny's Tip

USING BOLD PAINT STRATEGICALLY

Depending on the feel you want in a home office, you can go light and bright or dark and moody. Painting the space dark will make it feel a little more formal but won't make it feel smaller, contrary to what people often think. If you don't want to go all light or all dark, another option is to add wood paneling in a saturated color, with a lighter wall color above that adds visual interest and an appealing contrast.

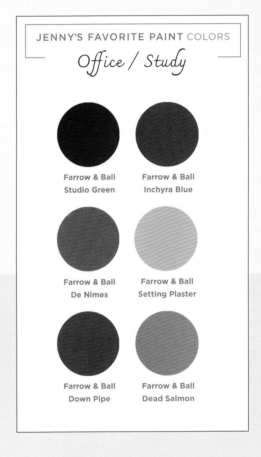

JENNY'S FAVORITE PAINT COLORS

Office / Study

Farrow & Ball
Studio Green

Farrow & Ball
Inchyra Blue

Farrow & Ball
De Nimes

Farrow & Ball
Setting Plaster

Farrow & Ball
Down Pipe

Farrow & Ball
Dead Salmon

WE ADDED TRIM AND three-quarter-height wall paneling to give this study an elevated look. I painted the trim and the doors the same shade to pull it all together, and across from the desk hung artwork created by the children of the house, bringing fun and color into the space.

ONE OF THE OWNERS of this house has been a writer for years, so I created a cozy writer's spot for her. Because this house is small, we wanted to maximize every single space, so Dave built a custom desk that can be hidden away when not in use. I enlisted the help of a calligrapher, who inscribed a message to remind Ashley to keep going "one word at a time."

Making & Doing

WE HAVE A ROBUST biking scene in our town, and the people who purchased this home decided to move here in part because of the access to bike trails. When we first discussed their remodel, they told us of future plans to build a garage at the back of the lot and we agreed to remove the old, dilapidated shed in their yard. However, once we inspected the shed, we found it in good condition so we decided to move it closer to the home, surround it with landscaping and a fire pit, and create a bike maintenance shop inside. Now they have a place to come home after a long day on the trails to work on their bikes and relax in front of the fire.

Dave

Making Things

I GREW UP in a really small town in Colorado. My brother, Matt, and I have always been around the building industry. My dad has been a builder for a long time, and he even built the house we lived in. My dad's also an incredible auto mechanic. Matt took to that more than to building, and I took more to the building and woodworking side, with woodworking becoming a passion of mine. At home, Mom and Dad encouraged me to be creative and to build whatever I could imagine. Like any good parent, they let me fail, figure it out, and create what I wanted. I didn't have the woodworking equipment at home that I have now in my shop, but Dad always had a table saw, a miter saw, and the basic tools I needed to build rudimentary furniture. In high school, I had great shop teachers. My high school shop was fully equipped with planers, sanders, paint rooms, and varnish rooms. It was where I could turn those two-by-four-foot tables I'd built out of scrap lumber from my dad's job site into hardwood pieces of furniture. My mom is one of those moms who likes to keep everything, so she still has a lot of the things I built in their house today, including a cedar end table and a checker/chessboard that my kids use when they visit.

The Shop

MY DREAM WAS to have a barn space like the one I have now. My barn shop is the fruition of ten years of working out of garages. Jenny and I moved from house to house as a builder and a builder's wife, and in those earlier houses, my shop was always the garage space, where I had only mobile tools—tools that could collapse and be shifted around—which limited me to working only on nice days when I could roll the planer out into the driveway without getting rained on.

In that time, I've refined my thinking about what I wanted as the centerpiece in my dream shop: the table saw. I use it more than any other tool. All the other tools are set up around the table, depending on how much I use them.

The Best Time of Day

MY IDEAL SHOP MORNING? Just before dawn, when it's still dark out, or when the sun's just coming up and it's snowing. I'll have a crackling fire going with a hot cup of coffee sitting atop the fireplace on a little grate I welded just for my mug. The smell of the logs burning alongside the smell of woodworking together with the aroma of steaming coffee in the quiet of the morning is like a little slice of heaven.

A Life Lesson from Building Houses

DON'T BE AFRAID to make mistakes. There are ten thousand different pieces that go into making a house and hundreds of different people who contribute to that house. If you get frozen by thinking that everything's not going to be perfect, you'll never get started. At the end of the day, building or renovating a house is literally just about sticks and bricks (or stones). Everything can be fixed. Everything can be modified. And sometimes that's where you find your greatest ideas—when things don't go as they're supposed to and you're able to bend and alter and change your ideas, so they come out better than you ever imagined.

CHAPTER 10

PLAYING, SLEEPING, LEARNING

SPACES FOR LITTLE ONES

—

Days of Summer

THE LAST DAY OF THE school year is one of my favorite days. As kids, my siblings and I would each invite a friend over for an end-of-the-year party that included our annual shaving cream fight. My mom would buy dozens of canisters of shaving cream and we would race home to throw on bathing suits and then gather in the yard, where my mom would dole out the cans. Shaving cream would fly through the air in a bizarre celebratory ritual as we laughed until our sides hurt. I don't know how my mom came up with this idea or remember when it started, but our annual shaving cream fights remain one of my most vivid and beloved childhood memories. My siblings, our closest friends from childhood, and I all carry on the tradition with our own kids to this day.

As summer approaches each year, I fill my shopping cart with watermelon and Popsicles, and I clear the grocery store's shelves of shaving cream. As I do, I feel the surge of joy that accompanies a calendar clear of sports practices and worksheets to sign and spelling words to review for a handful of glorious weeks. As a kid, summer break meant I could bask in the freedom of having nowhere to be and nothing to do. As a parent, summer break means no more nagging the kiddos to finish their homework before dinner. The absence of our normal frantic schedules invigorates their creativity and wild imaginations. My summer kitchen table is most often covered in my kids' art projects and dozens of paper airplanes. I make a deliberate choice to say no to overscheduling with activities and camps and sports, allowing them the freedom to explore in the woods and build forts with imaginary tunnels through the trees. Unhurried mornings create space for lingering on the front porch in pj's, coloring books strewn across the floor.

Summer is for unplanned, unhurried, unscheduled hours set aside simply to linger. To stoop down and scoop up a handful of wildflowers. To roam freely outdoors—awakening imaginations and senses gone dormant under academic and time pressure. To savor a new book from the library, saying yes to the enthusiastic request for one more chapter. To amble on a long walk down our quiet dirt road at dusk without the incessant pull to rush back home and complete the bedtime routine in preparation for another early morning.

Most important, this annual season of rest allows me to step back and evaluate what matters most to me as a mother. I ask myself: *If I imagine my grown children in twenty years, sitting around a table with their friends, how do I want them to describe their childhood?*

I know I want them to have fond memories of long days outside. I want them to remember dirt under their fingernails and laughter on their lips. I want them to remember the sensation of sunshine on their faces. I want them to remember the affection and responsibility they gleaned from caring for animals. I want them to remember a home with vases full of handpicked wildflowers on every surface and gallery walls covered in homemade Picassos. I want them to remember a childhood framed with sweet, content moments of lingering. I want them to have a solid foundation of tangible acts of love and a reservoir of joy to carry them throughout their lives.

We purposely moved to our farm in order to have the literal space for our kids to explore and be outside. We want them to activate the part of their brains that sparks imagination and learning through play. We are also intentional about ensuring there are creative opportunities for play throughout our home. We have a craft closet under our stairs, and we keep baskets of toys tucked on shelves and under tables throughout the house. As the kids get older, their needs change. Baby toys in the living room have been replaced with board games under the TV. I never tire of seeing a toy truck at work under the kitchen table or a family of dolls on the sofa.

Our house is not a museum. It's a living, breathing, soul-filling place where our kids learn what we value most. And we most value the five of them. If I value a perfectly orderly and clean home at all times, I can't possibly encourage art projects at the kitchen table. If I value quiet and serenity, I can't possibly embrace impromptu dance parties with music blaring and instruments being played. If I value a rigid schedule, I can't possibly be spontaneous and seek adventure. I want our home to be a place for new memories and old traditions to intertwine. I want it filled with the sweet sounds of laughter and celebration, as well as the mundane in-between moments that create a beautiful and full life.

NURTURING LITTLE PEOPLE INTO HAPPY, HEALTHY, CREATIVE, CARING BIG PEOPLE

Playing

THIS PLAYROOM WAS designed as a whimsical space for a family with three young kids. Dave built a quirky angled bookshelf as the focal point of the room, and I decided to carry the bold red of the painted circus-tent ceiling onto the bookshelf. This created a visually striking and imagination-inducing space that the kids absolutely loved.

Jenny's Tip

HIDDEN KITCHEN PLAYING SPACES

Every kid *loves* a hidden fort and every parent with young children *loves* a play area right near the kitchen so they can prep dinner in peace while the kiddos play happily nearby. Especially in older houses, there are often unused, awkward spaces where you can get creative in how you use them. They can become perfect play areas for little kids, and if you can make them "hidden," they're all the more fun. And when little kids become bigger kids and can no longer play in them, you can easily convert the spaces into storage areas.

WE DESIGNED THIS home with a family in mind and made room for a spacious pantry. I got creative with a large unused space

under the stairs right next to this kitchen I designed. A part of that space was too low and awkward to incorporate into the actual pantry, so I hid it with a door lined with shelving and then created a fun play area for kids.

I HAD TO THINK creatively when it came to a play area for the kids in this house. We discovered a large space under the staircase that could be the perfect spot for a tucked-away playhouse that would still be visible from the kitchen. We matched details from the exterior of the family's home to the playhouse façade, which gave the kids their own little home for playtime. We know how quickly kids can outgrow a play space, so we made the playhouse façade easily removable for when the time comes that they no longer want a playhouse in their kitchen.

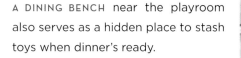

A DINING BENCH near the playroom also serves as a hidden place to stash toys when dinner's ready.

Jenny's Tip

HIDDEN STORAGE

I know I say it often, but it feels like you can never have enough storage, particularly when there are kids around. Whether it's drawers under a bunk bed or big baskets around to collect toys, being creative with solutions for where to put kids' stuff away is always top of our minds.

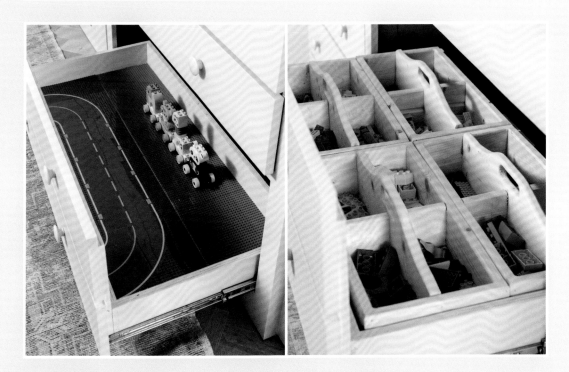

ONE OF THE KIDS in this family loves Legos, so instead of keeping them all stored away in his room, we used these drawers in a built-in so he could play with his Lego collection in the family room. The drawer keeps his creations safe from being stepped on and makes the Legos easy to clean up or hide away.

DAVE BUILT THIS scale model of the Welcome Inn for fun and we put it in the family suite in the house. The dollhouse has all the bedrooms of the real house and sits on a lazy Susan, so you can turn it easily. I found vintage dollhouse furniture, including a mini fridge. We thought it would be a fun opportunity for imaginative play when a family with kids is staying.

THIS BACKYARD WAS previously unused by the home-owners, and we knew we had to create a space for their son and daughter on the way to enjoy for years to come. Dave built a gorgeous A-frame playhouse that sits among the trees of the wooded backyard. It blends seamlessly with the surroundings and is an intentionally simple build that encourages creative play.

WE CREATED A screened-in porch for year-round use as a gaming room, a perfect spot for teenagers to play with friends or just hang out. Dave customized an old set of lockers to house all of the kids' gaming necessities, which took this dad-approved teenage hangout to a whole new level.

THE IDEA OF bringing a slide from the third-floor playroom down to the bedroom below was a little crazy but Dave Marrs managed to pull it off. We completed the slide with a little dock-inspired launch area. (See page 195 for a photo of the landing area in the bedroom below.) The top of the dock features a cozy nook for reading. The

climbing wall across the room is perfect for getting energy out. The gorgeous mural by a local artist completed the space—we move from the mountains of the Carolinas to the low country in this playroom. I wanted everything in this space to foster creativity, and for it to be a place where joyful childhood memories are made.

AT MY SISTER'S HOUSE, we created a comfy hangout and game room for my nephews. They'd recently moved to Northwest Arkansas after many years of living in Hawaii, so Dave handmade a surfboard as a nod to their previous home.

THE OWNERS OF this home recently moved from the Pacific Northwest and told us of their affinity for the sea and its wildlife. When we transformed the unused bonus room above the garage into a playroom and lounge area, Dave built a ship for their young son to play in, as a nod to their love of the ocean and to serve as the playful focal point of the space.

THE GIRLS IN this home like to craft, so Dave built a two-sided island where they each have their own space. The island is on wheels so that it can be easily moved, even to other places in the house. There are spots for each of them to sit, drawers for storage, and storage on the back wall, too, where we hung some of their art. We wanted it to be a space that encourages creativity.

Sleeping

TO BRING SOFT, pretty colors to this room, I chose muted pastels. The rainbow on the wall represents a promise, like the one given to Noah by God, because the baby who now occupies this room had been long-awaited and hoped for. My wish for this nursery was for it to be a visual symbol of the promise that joy always returns, even after suffering.

THIS BEDROOM NEEDED to have a wide doorway to accommodate a child who uses a wheelchair and a walker. Dave built a special bed, using the bed he made for our daughter Charlotte as a template. The tent-style structure could work for any child, but we kept it low to the ground for accessibility. We also kept the seating close to the ground, while the pink flamingo adds a cheery, eye-catching focal point.

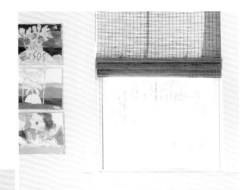

ALL ALONG, WE PLANNED this house for a family with kids. We knew that whoever ended up living here would want to live in a home that encouraged creativity and imagination and *fun*. This adorable beach-cottage playhouse bed and landing spot

from the upstairs slide is the perfect room for any kiddo. Our own kids even got in on the act and painted the artwork for this room. I love the warmth and coziness of the cedar shake siding on the playhouse and the adorable Dutch door that conceals the ladder up to the bed and landing area. This whole room is whimsical, and I absolutely adore it!

FOR THIS BUNK BED, we included storage drawers underneath and incorporated the ladder into the design, so it's not clunky and doesn't fall off. I found these enclosed nautical sconces that are easy for small hands to turn on and off. The little chair makes me smile, knowing how much a child will love it.

Learning

THE BREWER FAMILY needed this space to transition easily from school time to family time, so Dave built a home-school bookshelf with giant doors that hide the children's desks and supplies in order for the space to become a sophisticated living room once school hours are over.

WE CREATED THIS SIMPLE homework/
craft station with enough room for
three kids and versatile lighting options.
The large blackboard can easily be a
place for homework to-dos or a canvas
for creative chalk drawings. Our kiddos
added a few of their own colorful works
to the room.

Dave's Corner

TEACHING THE KIDS IN THE SHOP

The kids go through phases: The boys used to love being in the shop; now they kind of like videogames, but that's okay. These days the girls, and even Luke, are in the shop with me more often. I have scrap piles of lumber that are theirs for the taking. They'll come to me and say, "Hey, Dad, we want to build a table for our little fort outside." And so I'll help them with those kinds of things. We make stuff with handsaws, not power tools. It's amazing to see some of the stuff they've put together. The girls have built a few tables and they've built little desks for their closets. Luke and I built racetracks for his cars. We have bird-houses that they've con-structed hanging on trees. We even built a little man-ger for our Nativity scene. Anytime the kids want to be out in the shop with me, they're welcome; it gives Jenny a break and me some-one to talk to.

CHAPTER 11

RESTING

BEDROOMS, READING NOOKS & OTHER RECHARGING SPACES FOR BIG PEOPLE

———

Stillness

Corrie Ten Boom once said that if the devil can't make you sin, he'll make you busy. There's truth in that. Both sin and busyness have the exact same effect: They cut off your connection to God, to other people, and even to your own soul.

—**JOHN MARK COMER,** *The Ruthless Elimination of Hurry*

AS I'M TYPING THESE words, I have six tabs open on my computer, dozens of text messages to respond to, 231 unread emails, and a to-do list spanning three pages in my planner. My work schedule is the most demanding it's ever been, and I have approximately sixteen deadlines looming, with several dozen urgent decisions to be made by the end of the day. My kids' schedules also seem busier than ever, leaving me feeling like a taxi driver and personal concierge most days. Berry season is on the horizon with pressing needs that cannot be ignored, including pulling weeds and coordinating volunteer schedules.

While I know that there are many good things happening in my life, I also know that I feel a deep longing in my spirit for stillness and real rest. The reality of my current season is that I need to slow down. The irony of this is the fact that I'm typing these words in a hurry, as I have a conference call in fifteen minutes and have to be at a jobsite in forty-five minutes. I'm still in pj's and Luke is sitting in my lap eating cereal. I need to get him dressed and get myself ready so we can be out the door in exactly twenty-five minutes in order to be on time for the site visit. No doubt we will be running late and rushing out the door.

Yet, even amid a never-ending onslaught of demands on my time, I know I can find pockets of stillness right here in the midst of my real life. I don't need to run away to a private island. I don't need to quit my job and pull our kids from sports teams. I simply need to relearn the art of abiding. I need to truly engage in the sacredness of unplugging and resting. I need to turn off electronics and read a book, feeling the weight of it in my hands, turning the crisp pages instead of scrolling. I need to walk away from the to-do list and step into the pasture, relishing in the moment when sheep run toward me seeking treats, and our donkey, Daddy Donk, nuzzles against me as I brush his coat. I need to unplug from the hectic pace of our culture and gather with friends around the table, sharing a meal while the kids run outside, laughter spilling in through open windows along with the warm breeze.

I need to start the day in prayer, asking for wisdom and discernment over the needs of the day ahead. I need to pause to look my kiddos in the eyes while they are talking, watching as their faces light up with delight. I need to take deep breaths, pausing to tally my many reasons for gratitude. I need to extend myself grace, fully aware that this journey of eliminating hurry is a lifelong one.

Dave and I are similar in many ways, but when it comes to this idea of rest, we are polar opposites. My soul seeks stillness and my body physically feels worn down after a period of frenzied activity in a nonstop schedule. Dave, on the other hand, essentially refuses to be still. If we go on a vacation to the beach, I can lie on the sand with a good book for hours while he gets antsy after a few minutes and starts pacing the shoreline. At home, while I can sit by the fire and read or journal, Dave finds his place of soul rest while working with his hands out in the shop, and he is closest to God while on a tractor plowing the fields. Focused on a specific task at hand, Dave can be present and release the constant barrage of nonstop communication and pressing needs. He can quiet the noise of the world from his tractor cab and simply be. The way his soul is restored in the fields is just another reason I love this little farm of ours.

The truth is, there will be more seasons of overwhelm when I need a reminder to slow down, and there will be seasons when intentionally slow living comes easily and rest is tangible. No matter the season, I've learned the importance of carving out spaces in our home specifically for rest. For me, those spaces are the comfy chair where I can read next to the roaring fire in the winter or the porch swing where I can lean against oversized pillows and listen to the birds sing in springtime. I don't need to overhaul my home to create a cozy little spot, I simply need to light a candle, pour myself a steaming mug of coffee, and exhale. Most important, I need to give myself permission to be present and remember that the world will keep on spinning if I check myself out of the race for an hour. God doesn't need me to hold the world on my shoulders. He's got this. I can rest.

Intention

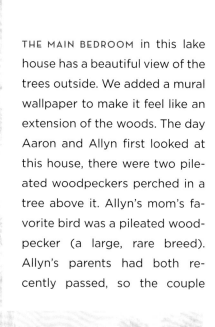

THE MAIN BEDROOM in this lake house has a beautiful view of the trees outside. We added a mural wallpaper to make it feel like an extension of the woods. The day Aaron and Allyn first looked at this house, there were two pileated woodpeckers perched in a tree above it. Allyn's mom's favorite bird was a pileated woodpecker (a large, rare breed). Allyn's parents had both recently passed, so the couple

took the birds as a sign that this was the house for them. I commissioned an artist to paint two woodpeckers directly onto the wallpaper in the same muted color scheme, and I added a natural woven light pendant for texture. The owners love the look of driftwood, so Dave built the nightstands out of driftwood we collected from the lake. The natural elements reflect the gorgeous nature outside, and everything about the room is serene.

THIS WAS THE ORIGINAL main bedroom in the Welcome Inn. When we bought the house, the room had an old, pretty pink floral wallpaper, but it was damaged and out of date. We wanted to take what was there and give it a fresh spin, so I commissioned an artist friend to create this wallpaper. I wanted larger-scale florals with more white space between them and a really soft, subtle pink tone to give the feel of the original bedroom with a modern update. Dave built the bed, with the rounded, welded headboard that is open at the back and doesn't block the wallpaper. The iron of the bed contrasts with the floral wallpaper really well, helping the room not to feel too heavy or overly feminine.

Jenny's Tip

BEDROOM WINDOW TREATMENTS

In a bedroom, I prefer curtains to shades because they soften the space. Though sometimes I'll layer natural woven shades with curtains to add extra texture. In kids' rooms, I like to use roman or woven shades. For curtain length, I prefer them to touch the floor and puddle slightly. I always hang the curtains as high as possible to give the illusion of more height in the room.

THIS HOME IS situated on a lake, so I wanted the overall space to feel natural and light. I used natural-fiber lighting with a woven texture and light-colored wood for the bed. The soft colors in the furnishings and the art enhance the light and airiness of the lakeside setting.

THIS IS A VERY simple, cozy bedroom. The room has low ceilings and since there was not a lot of space to work with, we added the slatted back wall to bring in height and add warmth and texture. The platform bed complemented the slatted wall, and the sconces add visual interest and help to define the wall as a focal point.

THIS BEDROOM HAS a low ceiling, which I accounted for by adding wall molding and a serene wallpaper to draw the eye upward and create the illusion of more space. Dave built the bed and nightstands to feel like vintage pieces that complement the classic and historically inspired design of this room.

JENNY'S FAVORITE PAINT COLORS

Bedroom

Farrow & Ball
Pointing

Farrow & Ball
Lamp Room Gray

Farrow & Ball
Light Blue

Benjamin Moore
Dusty Road

Farrow & Ball
Green Smoke

Farrow & Ball
French Gray

Sherwin-Williams
Doeskin

Benjamin Moore
White Dove

Farrow & Ball
Jitney

Sherwin-Williams
Gossamer Veil

Farrow & Ball
Blue Gray

Dave's Corner

CREATING FEATURE WALLS USING MOLDING

For a bedroom, you can add visual sophistication by using molding on a wall to create wainscoting with whatever pattern and at whatever height you want. It's inexpensive to do and it's a great way to create a feature wall. The shape of the molding really depends on what look you are going for. For example, picture-frame molding gives a more elevated feel.

Adding Molding to a Wall

Materials list for a twelve-foot wall:
- Three 16-foot sticks of panel molding
    (also known as accent molding)
- One 12-foot stick of chair rail molding
- One small tube of wood glue
- One tube of construction adhesive
- Blue snap-back chalk
- Miter saw

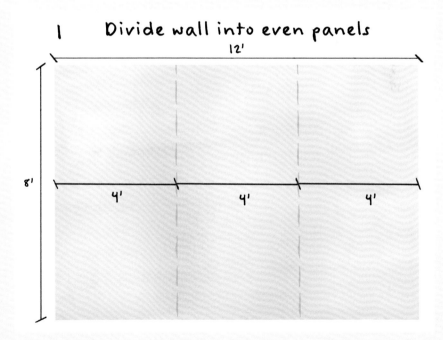

1   Divide wall into even panels

1. The first thing I do is measure the wall, dividing it evenly.
   If I've got a 12-foot wall, I break it up into three 4-foot panels.

(continued on next page)

2   Use blue chalk to snap out lines

2. I use blue chalk to outline the positions of my panels and chair rail on the whole wall before I make a single cut. That way, when I look at the wall with my blue chalk outline, if I don't like something, I can simply wipe it off and start over.

3. I cut the accent molding using a miter saw set at a 45-degree angle. Then I get my levels and put together my molding boxes—frames made of the accent molding you have chosen. They all need to be consistent sizes: You don't want to look at a wall and have three 2-foot-wide rectangles and one 3-foot-wide rectangle at the end.

3   Cut box frames and glue before you nail to chalk lines

4   Add upper chair rail

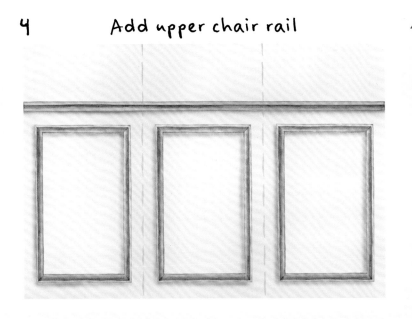

4. Nail the boxes to the chalk lines, then measure the distance from the bottom of the box to the floor and match that distance from the top of the box to the placement of the upper chair rail. Cut the chair rail molding to fit with your miter saw, then nail and glue to the wall.

5   Prime and Paint

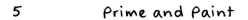

5. For a different look, you can set pieces of molding horizontally at a specific height of, say, one half or three-quarters of the way up the wall. Using your level again, place the pieces with glue and nail them horizontally along the wall. Then you can prime and paint the walls above and below the molding pieces to give different effects, depending on the look you are going for.

WE PLANNED THIS home for a family, and we wanted this beautiful main suite to serve as a retreat for the mom and dad. I wanted the calm, soothing, and peaceful aesthetic so characteristic of the Low Country to infuse the space. Every piece in this main suite was custom and hand-built by Dave. The color choices flow with the rest of the home, while the light wood and natural fiber furnishings add to the calming vibe.

WE CARVED OUT this little nook from a closet area off the main bedroom suite. We used three-quarter-height siding with soft wallpaper to add sophistication and interest. I visualized a young mother here snuggling with her baby or reading a book with her toddler tucked in the crook of her arm.

AARON AND BROOK, the owners of this bedroom, have young kids and were about to welcome a new baby, so I wanted this room to be elegant and a place to retreat. We added picture-frame trim and painted the whole room in a calming pewter. The window bench added a potential reading nook, though I imagined that with their baby on the way, it could be used as a convenient place to feed the newborn in the middle of the night.

SUZANNE LOVES TO READ. So Dave spent hours onsite in this serene bedroom building her a custom, cozy reading corner with a cushioned bench and a shelf for her books.

THIS LIGHT-FILLED READING nook sits at the top of the landing in the Welcome Inn. I kept the gallery wall behind it fairly simple, using a similar frame style and color palette. The photos within the frames are shots of the house from other eras, adding both historical context and a calming neutral scheme to what might have been an unused area.

Jenny's Tip

HANGING A GALLERY WALL

Gallery walls are a great way to feature treasured photos, heirlooms, and beautiful, interesting works of art. The mixing and matching of frames, art, photograph styles, and thematic content is appealing to the eye. Gallery walls work well in many places, including staircases—though for narrow spaces and hallways I more often use single large prints so that there is less for passersby to knock into.

I know there are oft-quoted rules for hanging gallery walls, but I don't really believe in those. I suggest just using what you love that you want to display.

A simple process I use to hang a gallery wall is as follows:

1. I lay out the various pieces I want to display on the floor. It's easiest to start in the center and work my way out. I like to have equal distance between frames, with different sizes, some vertical, some horizontal. Then I play around with sizes, shapes, and scales until I like the layout.

l Materials

2. Once I have a layout I like, I stack the frames to the side so that I don't step on them as I move around the room.

3. I lay out big sheets of Kraft paper on the floor and place the frames on the sheet in the configuration I like.

4. I trace an outline of the frames onto the Kraft paper and then remove the frames again.

5. I hang the Kraft paper onto the wall where I want it to go.

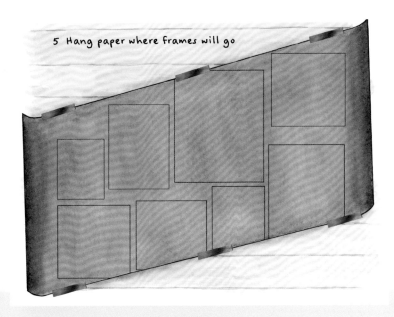

6. Using a measuring tape, I measure the distance from the top edge of each frame to the center of the frame wire, pulling the wire enough so that it is the approximate distance from the top edge that it will be when hung.

7. Matching that distance from the edge of the outline to the top of the frame wire, I tap my nail at the spot that will allow the piece to hang at the height of its outline. You can test your positioning by hanging the frame. It might take a little patience and adjusting to find the right nail positioning.

8. Once all the nails are in, pull the Kraft paper off, and you're ready to hang your frames on the nails.

Dave

The Finishing Touch

ON FLAGS

Hanging the flag at a house is always the last thing Jenny and I do in any renovation. Why? First of all, I love our country, though we have our problems just like any other country. Also, my dad was a veteran, and we have a lot of veterans in our family. They served our country, and we are a free place because of them. So we always hung an American flag on our house when we were growing up. I feel like the flag is a symbol of pride—of national pride. A flag can remind us of a time when we were more together: more of a family, more of a community. So it is very important to me.

Whether it stays up is not for me to decide, but I want to leave the flag there as an option for people. We get negative comments now and then, but many more people have said thank you for putting up the flag than have asked why we're putting it up. A flag hanging on the front porch says to everyone passing by: We're all in this together.

CHAPTER 12

DREAMING, CONTRIBUTING & CELEBRATING

OUT-IN-THE-WORLD PLACES

—

the Berry Farm

EACH YEAR IN MID-JUNE, we welcome several thousand people to our blueberry farm for our annual Berry Fest fundraiser. We work all year preparing for this event, with the final few weeks culminating in a flurry of activity. This year, while Dave and the boys were out mowing the fields and pulling the weeds, I was coordinating volunteer schedules and sending emails to encourage ticket sales. We created a map to designate food truck locations with pop-up shops

and kids' activity stations to be set up inside the barn. Shuttles were ordered and parking permissions were given by a neighboring school since their lot is clear for the summer. A stage and sound equipment were ordered and ready for the local musicians whose voices would carry through the fields as families picked berries.

As summer approached, our family headed out each evening after dinner to check the fields, just as we have done for

the past eight years. Pulling weeds and picking berries have framed our kiddos' summers for almost a decade now. Our kids have always jumped in and worked right alongside us. When we first planted the fields, Charlotte was a newborn. I strapped her to my back in a baby carrier and bent down to dig in the soil to plant two thousand blueberry and blackberry plants alongside Dave and the other kiddos. Three days after Luke was born, he was strapped into the same carrier as we welcomed families and handed out U-pick baskets for that summer's berry season. It's a beautiful privilege to be able to work as a family to grow delicious blueberries and to cultivate a space for our community to gather and experience a slice of farm life.

Most important, our small blueberry farm has taught us that we can do something bigger than ourselves. The mission of The Berry Farm is a domino effect rippling from Northwest Arkansas to Zimbabwe. Through our partnership with a nonprofit organization, our farm helps to fund an agricultural and vocational skills training program for orphaned and at-risk teens in rural Zimbabwe. This village and these kids are near and dear to our family, and we are blown away by the fact that our little farm tucked away here in the Ozarks is a part of bridging the gap for kids we love across the sea to transition successfully into adulthood.

This farm is one of the legacies Dave and I want to pass down to our children. We want them to value hard work and nature and, most of all, generosity. We want them to understand that it's never "us" and "them." It's not "here" and "there." We have had shared meals with our Zimbabwean leaders, at their table and at ours. We have become dear friends who do life together as best we can across an ocean. We hold them close in prayer and we have hopefully shown our kiddos that even though we live in different countries, with different cultures and foods and languages and looks, we are united in our humanity and our desire to run the race set before us well.

The work is hard and labor-intensive, but Dave and I believe it's worth every ounce of the sweat equity we have poured into these fields. There are so many hopes and prayers sewn into this soil, and when we finally welcomed old and new friends to the fields this past June for our annual event, it was, once again, a beautiful celebration. The sound of laughter as toddlers ran between the rows of blueberry plants, the sticky hands of kiddos who ate more berries than they placed in their baskets, and the joy of Luke, Charlotte, and Sylvie dancing on the bed of the blueberry truck are clearly etched in my mind, memories I will always cherish. My heart swelled with pride as I watched Ben and Nathan welcome guests to their annual Berry Good Lemonade stand set up at the edge of the barn. All weekend long, they hustled, running back and forth to the kitchen to make more lemonade or get more ice, never complaining about the heat or the hard work. At the end of each evening, they counted their earnings and donated half of the proceeds to the work happening in our beloved community in Zimbabwe.

I know that not everyone can go out and plant a blueberry farm in their backyard. But I do know that we can all intentionally create a home that fosters what we value most. If we ensure that our home is a place of generous hospitality, welcoming strangers and friends alike, we model a spirit of serving others for our watchful children. If we ensure that our home is a place of refuge and rest, welcoming friends and neighbors alike despite cultural, religious, or political differences, we model a spirit of unity in a divisive world. If we create a foundation at home that allows us to go out into the world and give of our time, our energy, and our resources, we model a spirit of generosity.

Dave and I often remind each other to remember our *Why*. It is the compass that guides every decision and every path we have set out on as a family. For us, The Berry Farm is at the heart of our *Why*. When we first stepped foot on foreign soil years ago and met starving children living in deplorable conditions, we knew we had to do something. Even if our something felt small and insignificant, we knew we had to try.

Over the next several years, we started

a feeding program for the kids we had met, sold our newly built Victorian house in our town's historic downtown, moved to the farm, adopted our daughter, partnered with John and Orpah, founded The Berry Farm, traveled to communities around the globe to learn best practices from leaders on the ground, worked with a local nonprofit here in our town to equip and provide resources to local foster families, and, probably the most familiar to many of you reading this book, we said yes to allowing cameras to document our lives.

In the spirit of full transparency, I can say we didn't initially want to be a part of a television show. We didn't want to lose privacy and expose ourselves to criticism. We didn't want to alter our children's lives or impact our already full schedules. Yet, we remembered our *Why*. We knew that the work of The Berry Farm—work we are passionate about—could be highlighted through a television show. We knew that if God gave us a platform to share about this work, more lives could be impacted and changed. So we said yes.

When the days are especially long or hard or the behind-the-screen critics are particularly harsh, Dave will simply look at me and say: "Remember *Why*." With that one word, my perspective shifts and my spirit settles. I know God doesn't need our family to do this work. Yet the fact that we get to be part of something so much bigger than ourselves is humbling, soul-gratifying, and life-giving. It's our unequivocal *Why*.

ACKNOWLEDGMENTS

I HAVE WANTED TO WRITE A book for as long as I can remember. This particular book has swirled around in my head in various forms for years and I doubt I would have been able to bring it to life without the wise counsel of my friend and book developer, Stephen Morrison. Stephen has provided guidance and edits and much-needed encouragement when the blank screen taunted me and my jam-packed schedule overwhelmed me into thinking this was an impossible pursuit. I'm forever grateful to both him and Su-sanna Lea for helping me navigate the world of publishing and, most of all, for believing in my words. And a warm thank-you to the entire team at Susanna Lea Associates, in particular Lauren Wen-delken and Helena Sandlyng Jacobsen.

While it still feels surreal to say the words "my publishing team," I am forever indebted to everyone at Convergent for working with me on this project: publisher Tina Constable, publicity director Cindy Murray, VP and deputy publisher Camp-bell Wharton, marketing director Jessalyn Foggy, senior marketing manager Rachel Tockstein, assistant publicity director Ste-ven Boriack, and so many more. To Keren Baltzer, thank you for making the pages of this book better. When we first met, I knew you would be the perfect editor because you believed in the message and, most impor-tant, you understand the value of recogniz-ing God's hand in the beauty that is so often overlooked in our lives. Keren's right hand, Leita Williams, has been an invalu-able support in putting this book together.

Barbara Bachman designed such a beautiful book, while production editor Loren Noveck and copy editor Liz Carbonell were clear-eyed and ever-helpful.

And, certainly, there wouldn't be a beautiful book filled with beautiful images of beautiful homes without the talented team I work with day in and day out. Lindsey Lustrino, thank you for being the other half of my brain. Words are insufficient to thank you for all that you do. Kim Brown, you give and give and give. You always have my back and I trust you implicitly with every home we work on. Thank you for saying yes to my crazy ask all those years ago. Melissa Halford, thank you for letting us take over your garage with packages and for running all over town ten times a day. You care deeply about these renovations and families, and that means the world to me. Sara Donahue, not only are you immensely talented, but you work hard and I can trust you to ensure that every detail is lovingly cared for. And I'll never forget the twenty-two-hour workdays we spent together in Charleston. I couldn't have done it without you. Corrie Rusch and Kristin Stehben, what a joy it was to work together on the Welcome Inn. Thank you for loving that old house as much as Dave and I do. Your love and care for it and for my vision is something I'll always be grateful for. Karey Marrs and Kennedy Marrs, you are

the best sister-in-law and niece I could ask for and you are both masters of closet styling. I love you both dearly. Rachelle Lazarro, I miss you and love that you were part of this team for a season of life. You are one of the very best. Jessica McNair, thank you for always being willing to do anything we need. Your generosity with your time and energy is invaluable. Laura Williams, you are the unsung hero of our work. Thank you for being flexible, kind, and gracious and for the years of hard work you have poured into these projects behind the scenes. Shea Frakes and Summer Shook, I adore you both and love our mornings together. You encourage me and point me to Truth and I am so thankful you have stepped into the crazy that is my life. Natalie Gebhart, thank you for agreeing to the enormous task that is caring for the guests at the Welcome Inn. You have the gift of hospitality, and it shines through your work.

Of course, there wouldn't be beautiful spaces to style without the incredible construction teams we work alongside. We have worked with many of these talented craftsmen for decades, and Dave and I both feel forever in their debt for the love, care, and talent they pour into every project. To Matt Marrs, Rob Nelson, Derek Hillyer, Chris Latham: Thank you for joining us on this journey. I know the timelines are absurd and I often make your lives miserable with my requests and changes, but you all are talented and gracious, and we couldn't do this without you. Thank you to Tom Stephenson for making floors look good all around Northwest Arkansas, to Dave Brown for ensuring hardware is installed exactly the way I want it, and to Tim Crawhorn for always agreeing to change the trim when I ask. Thank you to Joe and Chase Looney for all the laughs and memories over the years.

There aren't sufficient words to thank our production team at RIVR Media. Lori Stryer, you make me laugh every single day and our text messages give me life. Truly, you are also one of the smartest and most talented people I've ever worked with. Thank you for believing in us and for telling our stories so well. Thank you Stephanie Ellis and Angie Jedlicka for the endless hours of work and love you have poured into this show over the years. To the ones who have to sort through hundreds of hours of footage to make a show come together, Holly Markle and Andrew Jedlicka, thank you for your immense talent and for putting up with us all these years. Adam Neal, thanks for that cup of coffee that changed the course of our lives. Sarah Douglass, we miss you and love you and will never forget the way you cared for our family and this show so very well. Jeff Ross, welcome to the crazy train. Hold on

tight. Jerome Jernigan, Jason Bernardi, Grant Johnson, and Sam McDonald: You've watched our lives unfold from behind your lens for years now and we consider you an extension of our family. We are grateful for the very best team surrounding us every day.

To HGTV and Discovery, Inc. for consistently being in our corner and giving us a shot all those years ago. Carrie Regan, we still pinch ourselves that this is our life. You certainly have a very special place in our story and we adore you. Thank you for seeing something special here in Bentonville and in our family. To Matt Treweiler, you've made our show better with every decision and every question you ask us, and we respect and appreciate your wisdom and seemingly endless support. And to Betsy Ayala and Jane Latman, thank you for always believing in our work and supporting us so tirelessly.

To Cassidy Brust, words fail me. You are loved and appreciated beyond what I can type here. You care so well for the people I love most in this world. Thank you times infinity.

To the incredible homeowners and families we have worked with over the years, thank you for trusting us with your homes. We are humbled and grateful for the way you have allowed us to enter into your family's story and share it with others. We do not take this job of ours lightly—it has been a great honor to work with each of you.

An enormous thank-you to all of the makers, artisans, and artists who have contributed to our projects with loving attention to detail. We are extremely grateful for the way you each share your gifts with the world: Kelly Ventura, Rainy Bray of Fifth Pottery, Jason Pledger of Forever Design LLC, James Gardiner of Atmosphyre, Zu and Elyse of Zuma Imports, Mere Brown of Turkish Trunk, Tyler Burns of Ground Effects Landscaping, Jacob Hart of Sharums Landscaping, Jeff Lefever of TimberMill Wood Products, Matt Duboise of Carolina Coops, Dave Burris of Burris Architecture, Tammy Melton, Melissa Abide Griffith, Buddy Whitlock, Kinya Christian, J'Aaron Merchant, and Julie Wheeler.

To Mike Davello, this book quite literally wouldn't exist without you and your gorgeous photographs. Thank you for the time and energy and sacrifices you make.

To Adam Albright, the way you were able to capture our family and our life here on the farm through your lens is an absolute gift. I will always treasure your images of the people and the place I love most in this world.

Immense gratitude to the photographers who contributed to this project over the years. You each gave of your talent and time, and I hope I honored your work well within these pages: Rachelle Lazzaro, Samantha Daniels, Margaret Wright, Felecia Veazey, and Aaron Menken.

To Twilla Brooks, Dave and I are grateful for the work you do each day with the utmost care and attention. You have made our lives better. Thank you seems insufficient, but I also extend a lifetime of hugs in gratitude.

Thank you for the countless hours logging photos and Dropbox folders and files, Trian Koutoufaris. You have an eye for detail and a heart of kindness. I appreciate you so very much. Sophia Lacy and Bethany Carroz, you each add so much heart and talent to our team and our lives.

To Brian Samuels, thank you for always having our backs. You are deeply appreciated by both Dave and me.

Thank you to my biggest cheerleaders, the ones I group texted immediately when the contract was signed and then when I held the manuscript for the first time and when the final edits were turned in. The ones who have celebrated and encouraged and believed in this project from the very start. Brandy Becker and George Corton, I'm thankful you two have been my confidants and friends for all my life. Chanika Ogle, you are a bright light, my friend. Jennifer Armbruster and Andrea Young, thank you for walking tenderly beside me on some of the hardest roads, even from afar. And to my Farkles—Allie Wells, Beth Waldmann, Brianna Wells, Lauri Meidell, Lindsay Peattie, Molly Bottoms, and Vicki Calonge—you girls have loved me well for as long as I can remember. Thank you, thank you, thank you.

Immense gratitude goes to my parents, Joan and Steve, and my in-laws, Donna and David, for being the foundation of our family and tangible examples of how to love and live well.

To my siblings and their spouses— Angie and Rob, Lori and Bryan, Steven and Christina—I love you all so very much. Our family group texts make me smile, laugh, and cry—often at the same time. God broke the mold with our family. I am ridiculously blessed.

To my sisters- and brother-in-law— Bridget, Matt and Karey, and Katie, thank you for welcoming me so lovingly into the Marrs' fold. What an immense privilege it is to be a part of this beautiful family.

Most of all, thank you to my babies (don't roll your eyes; you'll always be my babies): Ben, Nathan, Sylvie, Charlotte, and Luke. You five have taught me everything I need to know about being creative and brave. Going on adventures with you all is my favorite thing to do. Thank you for showing me how to seek beauty all around me. You each make this world a brighter place, and watching you grow has been the single greatest joy of my life.

And of course, to Dave: I never would have written this book without your encouragement and loving persistence that I *can* do this. You believe in me more than I believe in myself, and I will always be grateful that you do. Loving you is my favorite thing to do. Thank you for making it so easy. Here's to our most abundantly beautiful life together. Cheers, my love.

PHOTO & ILLUSTRATION CREDITS

PHOTOGRAPHS

Courtesy of Aaron Menken: pages 232 (top row, center, and bottom left), 233 (all)

Courtesy of Adam Albright: back cover, front endpaper; pages ii, xii, xix, 2, 20, 39, 40, 43, 45, 56, 58, 90, 92–93 (all), 102, 120 (right), 122–123 (all), 126, 148, 180, 199, 200

Courtesy of Danielle Keller: pages 128–29 (all)

Courtesy of David Brown: back endpaper

Courtesy of Felecia Veazey: page 230

Courtesy of Jenny Marrs: pages xxii-1, 4–5 (all), 14, 16 (all), 63, 88, 104–05 (all), 106, 168–69 (all), 179, 183, 226, 228 (all), 232 (bottom right)

Courtesy of Karey Marrs: page 23

Courtesy of Kelly Ventura: page 164 (all)

Courtesy of Margaret Wright: pages 96, 100, 108–09, 154 (right), 158 (right), 163, 185 (all), 190 (all), 195 (all), 198 (all), 216–17 (all)

Courtesy of Michael Howard: page 140 (bottom)

Courtesy of Mike Davello: front cover; pages xiv (all), 7, 8–9 (all), 10–11 (all), 17, 19 (bottom), 26, 28 (all), 29, 34, 36, 37, 38, 46–47, 48, 49, 50, 52–53 (all), 55, 64–65, 66 (all), 67, 68–69 (all), 70, 71 (all), 72, 73 (top), 74–75 (all), 76–77 (all), 80–81 (all), 82–83 (all), 84–85 (all), 86–87 (all), 89 (all), 98–99 (all), 101, 110–11, 112–13 (all), 114–15, 116–17 (all), 118–19 (all), 120 (left), 121, 124–25 (all), 136–37 (all), 139 (all), 140 (top), 141, 142 (all),

143 (all), 144–45 (all), 146–47 (all), 152–53 (all), 154 (left), 155 (all), 156–57 (all), 158 (left), 160–61 (all), 162, 165 (all), 166, 173 (all), 174–75 (all), 176–77 (all), 178, 184 (all), 187 (all), 188 (left), 189 (all), 191 (all), 192–93 (all), 194 (all), 196–97 (all), 204–05 (all), 206–07 (all), 208–09 (all), 210–11 (all), 212, 218–19 (all), 220, 225, 242 (all)

Courtesy of Rachelle Lazzaro: pages 12–13 (all), 73 (bottom), 132–33, 170–71 (all), 186 (all), 188 (right)

Courtesy of Samantha Daniels: pages 18, 19 (top), 134–35 (all), 138 (all)

ILLUSTRATIONS

Schematics courtesy of Bethany Carroz: pages 31–33, 78–79, 213–15, 221–23

Paint charts courtesy of Sophia Lacy: pages 71, 143, 172, 211

ABOUT THE AUTHORS

JENNY MARRS is a designer, writer, and passionate advocate for community transformation, family preservation, and orphan care around the globe. She is married to Dave, and they live on a small farm in Bentonville, Arkansas, with their five kids and too-many-to-count animals.

DAVE MARRS is an expert craftsman, furniture builder, and general contractor. He is also a self-taught farmer, cofounding The Berry Farm along with his wife, Jenny.

In partnership with HGTV, Jenny and Dave developed *Fixer to Fabulous,* a home renovation show focused on restoring historic homes in their beautiful Northwest Arkansas area.

Instagram: @jennymarrs
@dave.marrs
@daveandjennymarrs
daveandjennymarrs.com

ABOUT THE TYPE

This book was set in Caslon, a typeface first designed in 1722 by William Caslon (1692–1766). Its widespread use by most English printers in the early eighteenth century soon supplanted the Dutch typefaces that had formerly prevailed. The roman is considered a "workhorse" typeface due to its pleasant, open appearance, while the italic is exceedingly decorative.